Skills for **Employability**

StepUP

B2+

Coursebook and **eBook**

Aslıhan Çelik
Yeşim Kırlı
Robyn Brinks Lockwood
Nancy Blodgett Matsunaga

Step Up B2+

Pearson Education, 221 River Street, Hoboken, NJ 07030 USA

Cover Illustration: Roy Hermelin

Text composition: Straive

Library of Congress Cataloging-in-Publication Data: A catalog record for the print edition is available from the Library of Congress.

Printed in the United States of America

ISBN-13: 978-0-13-747369-4

1 2023

Acknowledgments

We would like to thank the following people for their help with this project.

Güzide Göksen Birol, Istanbul Okan University; **Eduardo Pinell Campuzano,** CIU Director, Universidad Privada Franz Tamayo; **Meg Cassamally,** University of Siena; **Adrian Crawley,** Evority Learning Centre; University of Siena; **Yabancı Diller,** School of Foreign Languages; **Louise Dixon,** Director of Studies at Hallo! Servizi Linguistici; **Aybala Eren,** Gazi University; **Alex Fayle,** Well & Will Language Academy; **Elizabeth Cruz Flores,** Tecnológico de Monterrey; **Jacques Friggieri,** Redrob; **María Amparo Garcia,** ICPNA Cusco; **Christina Gebbia,** Director of Let's Talk English Center in Valencia; **Maria de la Paz Giglio,** New Concept School of English; **Zeynep Güler,** İstanbul Okan University; **Ilaria Incorvaia,** ITIS 'Antonio Meucci', Florence; **Nancy Johnstone,** School of Engineering, UBA, Buenos Aires, Argentina; **Sevil Altıkulaçoğlu Kayaer,** Gazi University; **Yeliz Korkmaz,** Yıldız Technical University, Turkey; **Héctor Raúl Sánchez Lozano,** Proulex Universidad de Guadalajara; **Mariana Juana Aviles Martillo,** coordinator of CEFI, Center for Continuing Educatiòn and Interamerican Labor; **Anne Marie Mc Gowan,** University of Rome ' Tor Vergata ' Italy; **Cristian Meléndez,** Universidad Católica de El Salvador; **Jose Manuel Mendivil S.,** Centro Boliviano Americano - Fundación Cultural y Educativa La Paz; **Paul Cruz Montenegro,** English Coordinator of CRC - Peru Cruceros; **M.Àngels Nogué,** Centre D'Idiomes Olot; **Irem Ozcan,** Gazi University, College of Foreign Languages; **Claudia Posarelli,** ITIS Meucci Firenze; **Steven Pragnell,** Astex Servicios Lingüísticos, Madrid; **María de Lourdes Camarillo Rodríguez,** Escuela Bancaria y Comercial; **Raquel Sánchez,** Faculty of Education in Albacete (UCLM); **Chayapak Tangapiwut,** Burapha University Language Institute; **Onur Uludag,** Yildiz Technical University; **Taku Umeda,** Tokyo Business and Language College; **Laura Vacca,** Inglese su Misura; **Marijke van Leuven,** Oxford School of English, Verona, Italy.

Photo Credits Page 2: Shutterstock; 5: Fizkes/Shutterstock; 7 (A): Andrey_Popov/Shutterstock; 7 (B): Wavebreakmedia/Shutterstock; 7 (C): Srdjan Randjelovic/Shutterstock; 7 (D): Fizkes/Shutterstock; 7 (E): Wavebreakmedia/Shutterstock; 7 (F): MS_studio/Shutterstock; 8 (shaking head): Sruilk/Shutterstock; 8 (curling finger): Natalya Erofeeva/Shutterstock; 8 (eye contact): True Touch Lifestyle/Shutterstock; 9: Fizkes/Shutterstock; 11 (Scenario 1): SofikoS/Shutterstock; 11 (Scenario 2): LDprod/Shutterstock; 11 (Scenario 3): Shutterstock; 13: Nejron Photo/Shutterstock; 14 (Scenario 1): Stockfour/Shutterstock; 15 (Scenario 2): Antoniodiaz/Shutterstock; 15 (Scenario 3): Fizkes/Shutterstock; 15 (Grace): Stockfour/Shutterstock; 15 (Levi): Antoniodiaz/Shutterstock; 15 (Nova): Fizkes/Shutterstock; 16 (location icon): Treter/Shutterstock; 16 (weightlifter): Treter/Shutterstock; 16 (couple icon): Treter/Shutterstock; 16 (stethoscope icon): Treter/Shutterstock; 16 (roller brush icon): Treter/Shutterstock; 16 (microscope icon): Treter/Shutterstock; 16 (hot air balloon icon): Treter/Shutterstock; 16 (road sign icon): Treter/Shutterstock; 16 (internet icon): Treter/Shutterstock; 17: George Rudy/Shutterstock; 18: Pressmaster/Shutterstock; 19: LightField Studios/Shutterstock; 20 (heart and brain): Sylverarts Vectors/Shutterstock; 20 (soft skills): Anton Shaparenko/Shutterstock; 20 (emotional intelligence): LvNL/Shutterstock; 20 (professionalism): Jiris/Shutterstock; 20 (emotion and intelligence balance): InimalGraphic/Shutterstock; 21: ImageFlow/Shutterstock; 23 (scenario 1): Takayuki/Shutterstock; 23 (scenario 2): Sarayut Sridee/Shutterstock; 24 (female avatar): Voysla/Shutterstock; 24 (male avatar): Voysla/Shutterstock; 25: Fizkes/Shutterstock; 27 (A): Fizkes/Shutterstock; 27 (B): Fizkes/Shutterstock; 27 (C): Patpitchaya/Shutterstock; 27 (D): Song_about_summer/Shutterstock; 27 (E): Fizkes/Shutterstock; 28 (Jacinda Ardern): Photocosmos1/Shutterstock; 28 (Steve Jobs): Jaguar PS/Shutterstock; 28 (Sadhguru Jaggi Vasudev): Madhuram Paliwal/Shutterstock; 29: Makistock/Shutterstock; 31 (scenario 1): Vadym Pastukh/Shutterstock; 31 (scenario 2): Prostock-studio/Shutterstock; 32 (avatar): Sapann Design/Shutterstock; 32 (avatar): Sapann Design/Shutterstock; 32 (avatar): Sapann Design/Shutterstock; 32 (avatar): Sapann Design/Shutterstock; 32 (avatar): Sapann Design/Shutterstock; 32 (avatar): Sapann Design/Shutterstock; 33: PR Image Factory/Shutterstock; 34: Mix and Match Studio; 35 (Form 1, Karl): Krakenimages.com/Shutterstock; 35 (Form 2, James): Krakenimages.com/Shutterstock; 35 (Form 3, Luna): Roman Samborskyi/Shutterstock; 36: Jesus Sanz/Shutterstock; 37: Stoatphoto/Shutterstock; 39 (scenario 1): Baranq/Shutterstock; 39 (scenario 2): Batkova Elena/Shutterstock; 39 (scenario 3): Ground Picture/Shutterstock; 40: BRO.vector/Shutterstock; 41: Gorodenkoff/Shutterstock; 42: Takayuki/Shutterstock; 43: Michaeljung/Shutterstock; 44: Graphicwithart/Shutterstock; 45: Rawpixel.com/Shutterstock; 47: Ground Picture/Shutterstock; 48 (top): Marta Sher/Shutterstock; 48 (bottom): TeraVector/Shutterstock; 49: Fizkes/Shutterstock; 50 (scenario 1): Baranq/Shutterstock; 51 (scenario 2): Dragon Images/Shutterstock; 51 (scenario 3): Kateryna Onyshchuk/Shutterstock; 52 (top left): Inspiring/Shutterstock; 52 (top center left): Naum/Shutterstock; 52 (top center right): VZ_Art/Shutterstock; 52 (top right): Sagii/Shutterstock; 52 (bottom left): Inspiring/Shutterstock; 52 (bottom center left): GoodStudio/Shutterstock; 52 (bottom center right): Yellow_man/Shutterstock; 52 (bottom right): LanKogal/Shutterstock; 74 (woman and man avatars): Gurza/Shutterstock; 76: Upstudio/Shutterstock; 78: Sofam/123RF; 79 (Danielle avatar): Sudowoodo/123RF; 79 (Anders avatar): Sudowoodo/123RF; 79 (Martina avatar): Sudowoodo/123RF; 79 (Akhil avatar): Sudowoodo/123RF; 79 (Jada avatar): Sudowoodo/123RF; 79 (Kazue avatar): Sudowoodo/123RF; 80 (woman and man avatars): Gurza/Shutterstock; 81 (woman avatar): Gurza/Shutterstock; 82 (woman and man avatars): Gurza/Shutterstock; 83: Vmaster/Shutterstock; 85 (Tracy): Jossnat/Shutterstock; 85 (Mandy): Jossnat/Shutterstock.

Scope and Sequence

Welcome page 2	In the classroom | Learn about your book | Meet your Employability Skills Coaches

Module	I can . . .	Learning Objectives	Vocabulary
1 **Communication 1** Nonverbal Communication pages 5–8	I can explain how to use and interpret nonverbal communication professionally	• Explain the importance of nonverbal communication in the workplace • Identify common types of nonverbal communication • Recognize how to interpret nonverbal communication correctly • Explain how to avoid misinterpreting nonverbal communication	*assert, detect, differ, eyebrows, focused, transpose, frown, interpret, preferred, sincere, transmission, unsure of yourself*
2 **Communication 2** Persuasive Communication pages 9–12	I can describe ways to develop my persuasive communication skills	• Describe the benefits of using persuasive communication at work • Recognize the main tools and principles of persuasive communication • Identify ways to develop persuasive communication skills	*anecdote, credible, empathize, entrepreneur, friendliness, likeable, persuasive, pitch, prompt, prospective, reluctant, trustworthy*
3 **Goal Setting** Sticking to Your Goals pages 13–16	I can describe specific strategies for staying committed to my goals	• State the importance of setting and committing to goals • Explain why committing to goals can be difficult • Identify strategies to stay committed to goals	*align with, buddy, challenging, payoff, pressure, resilient, sabotage, see (something) through, self-confidence, self-talk, stick to (something)*
4 **Teamwork** Building Emotional Intelligence pages 17–20	I can explain what emotionally intelligent teams look like and the benefits of them	• Describe the components of emotional intelligence and how they contribute to success in the workplace • Identify the attributes of a successful team with emotional intelligence • Identify ways to build an effective team with emotional intelligence	*awareness, diffuse, exhibit, fuel, gratifying, hesitant, interdependence, intrinsic, perceive, praise*
5 **Critical Thinking** Decision Making pages 21–24	I can explain the seven steps to effective decision making	• Explain the difference between low-risk and high-risk decisions • Identify the seven steps in the decision-making process • Discuss the common myths about decision making	*alternative, consider, decision making, gather, high-risk, indecisive, intuition, low-risk, outcome, weigh*
6 **Leadership** Leadership Styles pages 25–28	I can describe the five common leadership styles	• State the importance of developing a leadership style • Describe five common leadership styles and when they work most effectively • Identify ways to develop a leadership style	*authoritarian, autonomy, boost, charismatic, commitment, consensus, delegate, dominant, hands-off, manipulate, mentoring, neglected*

Pronunciation	Language Strategy	Project	Talk!
The *-ed* ending in adjectives	Understand the main points of presentations: Signposting language	Focus on own facial expressions and gestures	Explore cultural differences in body language
Weak pronunciation of object pronouns	Identify key details in a linguistically complex text	Online research of Cialdini's principles of persuasion	Discuss whether storytelling, providing data, or both combined are most persuasive
The letter *a*	Differentiate between genuine and rhetorical questions	How to stay committed to professional and personal life goals	Popular life goals
Main stress in sentences	Understand connotations	Create a survey on challenges when working in teams	The role of emotional intelligence in the workplace
Stressed syllables in nouns	Anticipate ideas	Research and make a list of additional tips for how to achieve work-life balance	Negative consequences of overthinking decisions
The letter *s*	Recognize contrasting ideas signaled by discourse markers	Interview someone about their leadership style	Discuss some world-famous leaders' quotes

Pronunciation	Language Strategy	Project	Talk!
Consonant groups	Follow lines of argument	Create a plan to meet a deadline	Talk about setting and meeting deadlines
Syllables and stress	Understand idiomatic language	Make a list of additional tips for achieving work-life balance	The top five countries with the best work-life balance
Stress in compounds	Identify the purpose of questions	Apply the PLUS model to an ethical dilemma	Ethics in the workplace
Thought groups	Recognize the emphasis of significant points	Prepare an elevator pitch	Common mistakes made during an elevator pitch
Emphatic stress	Understand advice	Search for jobs on a professional networking site	Statistics on employers using social media to find suitable candidates
Stressed words	Understand complex language in discussions	Prioritize a list of criteria for evaluating a job offer	Which factors people consider before accepting a job offer

To the Teacher

Overview

Step Up is a flexible online course designed for adults or young adults who want to improve their employability skills—whether to get a first job, secure a promotion, find a different job, re-enter the workforce after an absence, or change fields. Although the emphasis of the course is on employability skills, *Step Up* also develops English language skills by providing vocabulary instruction and practice, listening, reading, and notetaking skills, pronunciation practice, and discussion strategies.

Levels

There are six levels of *Step Up*, CEFR A2+ to C1, Global Scale of English (GSE) 34 to 84.

***Step Up* level**	**GSE**
Step Up A2+	34–43
Step Up B1	41–51
Step Up B1+	49–58
Step Up B2	56–66
Step Up B2+	64–75
Step Up C1	73–84

Two Versions of *Step Up*

Students can study the *Step Up* course in two ways: as a self-study course or as a self-study plus course, which is the self-study course combined with a teacher-led class. As a self-study course, each level of *Step Up* takes students 18 hours to complete, though this may vary as it is self-paced. The teacher-led course provides 14 hours of class time, with additional resources and extension activities available in the Teaching Notes, which would extend class time.

Student's Components

	Self-study course	**Self-study plus course**
Online Course	✓	✓
Coursebook + eBook or eBook only	✗	✓
Resources (online)	✓	✓

Teacher's Components

	Self-study plus course
Coursebook and/or eBook	✓
Access to the Online Course	✓
Teaching Notes	✓
Resources (online)	✓

The Online Course

Students study the following 12 modules, of which the first nine are **personal and social capabilities** and the last three are job-seeking skills:

Module 1 Communication 1	**Module 2** Communication 2	**Module 3** Goal Setting
Module 4 Teamwork	**Module 5** Critical Thinking	**Module 6** Leadership
Module 7 Self-Management	**Module 8** Wellness	**Module 9** Social Responsibility
Module 10 Branding	**Module 11** Job Search	**Module 12** Interviewing

Each module has an employability skills coach—an animated character—who takes the students through the 10 steps of the module. Step 11 is a progress check; it includes a practice test and a graded test. If the student scores at least 70% on every graded test, they are given access to the final exam. If they score at least 80% on this assessment, they receive a certificate of completion.

For a closer look at the online course, please see the Online Module Walkthrough in the Teacher Resources.

Coursebook/eBook

The Coursebook/eBook is made up of two main sections: the modules and the back matter.

The Modules

Welcome module

The Coursebook begins with a Welcome module, which is comprised of four sections to:

- help students get to know each other and form a community of learners
- provide students with useful language they need to work effectively in class
- help students navigate the Coursebook so they get the most out of it
- introduce students to the 12 employability skills coaches they meet in the online course.

The 12 Employability Skills Modules

Following the Welcome module are the 12 employability skills modules, corresponding to each module in the online course. Students need to do each online module before they come to class. In class, you guide them through each module to reinforce what they have learned online, to deepen their understanding of the material, and to share how they can apply what they have learned to their own lives.

Back Matter

There are four sections in the back of the Coursebook and eBook:

- *Check your understanding* enables students to demonstrate they have understood the material they have studied online and gives them an opportunity to clear up any misunderstandings at the beginning of a class.
- *Discussion strategies* provide students with four different sets of strategies that can help them engage in class. These include how to work with others; clarify what you hear or clarify what you say; get and stay involved in the discussion; and organize your ideas. Audio models enable students to practice their pronunciation.
- *Vocabulary practice* gives students additional practice with the vocabulary they have learned in the online course. The first activity is a word puzzle, and the second activity uses the target words from the puzzle in context. The answers are provided in the eBook and in the Resources folder.
- *The Glossary* provides the definitions of some words or phrases printed in light brown in the Coursebook to facilitate understanding.

Flexibility

While the sequence of the modules is fixed in the coursebook, you can change the sequence to meet the needs of your students. You may want to have the class review the scope and sequence and vote on which modules to do first. If you change the sequence, we suggest you create a syllabus and upload it to the platform.

Resources for Students

All audio and video files for the online course and all audio files for the coursebook are accessible within the activities in the course. In addition, these audio and video files are also available in the Resources, to allow students to watch or listen whenever they wish without going to the lesson itself. Also included in the Resources are the reading texts, as well as answer keys to the *Vocabulary practice* in the Coursebook.

Resources for Teachers

Teaching Notes

There are general teaching notes to help you get the most out of the course. Then there are notes for each module that begin with an overview of the online module that synopsizes what the students have learned online. Following the overview are teaching notes for each step in the coursebook, including tips, extensions, culture notes, and more.

Module Walkthrough

There is also a module walkthrough that visually describes a module and the underlying pedagogy for both the online course and the coursebook.

Platform Support

To help you navigate the platform and use all the tools available, there is a guided tour when you first log on to Pearson English Connect. In addition, you will find numerous resources under the "Help" button to orient you to the platform. And to get in touch with support, you can click on Help>Documentation>Contact Support.

Welcome

① In the classroom

A Get to know your classmates

Talk to your classmates. Find someone who matches each prompt. Write their first name on the line. Then ask follow-up questions.

- loves to read ____________
- has ridden a motorcycle ____________
- enjoys cooking ____________
- can play a musical instrument ____________
- has traveled to another country ____________
- is very artistic ____________

B Useful language

Here are some examples of strategies that will help you overcome challenges in discussions with classmates or colleagues. Complete the tips with the problems in the box.

~~**a** doesn't participate~~	**c** goes off topic	**e** speaks too softly
b speaks too quickly	**d** speaks too much	**f** interrupts others

☐ **1.** If someone doesn't participate, invite him or her to join in by saying things like ...
- "What do you think, Diego?"
- "We haven't heard from Chiyo yet. What do you think about ...?"

☐ **2.** If someone ____________, get him or her back on track by saying things like ...
- "Let's return to what Lanh was saying."
- "That's a good point, but let's get back to the main issue."

☐ **3.** If someone is impatient and frequently ____________, you can say ...
- "Wait your turn, please. You'll have a chance to talk in a moment."
- "Hold on. Let Malik finish what he's saying."

☐ **4.** If someone ____________ and others don't have the opportunity to speak, you can politely interrupt by saying ...
- "Thank you, Noor. Now let's hear what other people have to say."
- "That's an interesting idea. What do you think about that, Jae-jin?"

☐ **5.** If someone ____________, ask him or her to slow down by saying ...
- "Would you mind slowing down?"
- "Could you say that a little more slowly, please?"

☐ **6.** If someone ____________, and others have trouble understanding what is being said, get him or her to speak up by saying ...
- "Would you mind speaking up a little?"
- "I'm afraid we can't hear what you're saying."

C Discuss

PAIRS **Listen to a dialog and choose the strategies you hear from 1B. Which strategies are the most useful? Why?**

② Learn about your book

1 How many modules are in the course?

a 5 **b** 9 **c** 11 **d** 12

2 How many steps are in each module?

a 6 **b** 7 **c** 8 **d** 9

3 Look at this icon on page 5.
It tells you to go to page 68.
Read what is on that page.
How can you use that information?

DISCUSSION STRATEGIES

Go to page 68.

____

4 On page 5, Exercise C says Check your understanding. Go to page 54. What is on that page?

a questions to test vocabulary
b questions to ask my teacher
c questions to review the Online Course
d questions to ask my partner

5 Look through Module 1. Which Steps in the book refer to Steps in the Online Course?

a Steps 1, 2, and 3
b Steps 2, 5, and 7
c Steps 3, 4, and 6
d Steps 5, 6, and 7

6 Look at the I-can statement after Step 7 in each module, for example

I can identify successful communication skills. ☐

What is it for?

____

7 What will you find on pages 72–83?

a listening practice
b grammar practice
c vocabulary practice
d pronunciation practice

8 What will you find on pages 86–87?

a a glossary
b listening activities
c vocabulary practice
d an audio script

To find the answers for CHECK YOUR UNDERSTANDING and VOCABULARY PRACTICE you can look in your ebook or use the answer key in the Student's Resources online.

Meet your Employability Skills Coaches

MODULE 1
Greetings! I'm Dr. Jabu Cele. I have my doctorate in communications and I'm a senior vice president at one of the world's top marketing companies.

MODULE 2
Hi there! I'm Emma Lu, and I'll be your coach for the Communication 2 module. I'm a corporate teamwork coach.

MODULE 3
Hello there. I'm Zehra Teke and I'll be your Employability Skills coach for the module about Goal Setting. I'm a business consultant with a master's degree in management.

MODULE 4
Hello! My name is Kristine Ross. I'm the human resources manager for a large, international company. I'll be your coach for the Teamwork module.

MODULE 5
Hello. My name is Marek Kamiński. I'm an investigative journalist and I'll be your Employability Skills coach for the Critical Thinking module.

MODULE 6
Hi, I'm Sonia Lopez. I'll be your coach for the Leadership module. I'm the Chief Executive Officer—the CEO—of the Alacarte Restaurant Group.

MODULE 7
Hello, my name is Felix Becker. I'm a professional certified life coach and I'll be your coach for the Self-Management module.

MODULE 8
Hello and welcome to the Wellness module. I'll be your Employability Skills coach. My name is Kai Sugimoto. I have a PhD in psychology and I do research on health and wellness.

MODULE 9
Hello, there. My name is Ana Silva. I'm the coordinator of social responsibilty for a large company and I am your coach for the Social Responsibilty module.

MODULE 10
Hi, Welcome to the Branding module. I'm Rakesh Patel, and I'm your Employability Skills coach. I work in marketing.

MODULE 11
Hello! Welcome. I'm Justin Roy, and I'm your coach for the Job Search module. I'm a career advice blogger and my goal is to help people find their dream jobs.

MODULE 12
Hi. My name is Aisha Omar. I'm a career counselor at the U.S. Department of Labor and I'll be your coach for the Interviewing module.

MODULE 1

Communication 1

Nonverbal Communication

DISCUSSION STRATEGIES

Go to page 68.

Step 1 Get started

A Refresh your memory! Watch the *What You'll Learn* video.

B Look at the photo. What do you think these people are doing when you look at their body language? How do they feel? Do you pay attention to your body language? How?

C Check your understanding. Go to page 54.

Step 2 Tell your story

A THINK In your online course, you thought about a time that you misinterpreted nonverbal communication. What happened and how did you proceed? Listen to the example.

B PAIRS Discuss your story.

C SHARE Tell your story to the class.

Step 3 Take away

A THINK Review your notes from the online module and match the words with the definitions.

facial expressions | eye contact | physical distance | posture | gestures

Nonverbal Communication

Type	Definition	Examples
	when two people look at each other's eyes while communicating	
	the motions you make with the muscles in your faces	
	movements we make with our hands, arms, and heads	
	the space between people	
	the way we hold our bodies while sitting or standing	

B PAIRS For each of the descriptions, write 1-3 examples or notes.

C SHARE Check your answers with the class and add more examples to the descriptions.

Step 4 Activate your knowledge

A PAIRS Read the scenarios and look closely at the photos. Complete the chart with the body language you see and the message it communicates.

A

Dmitri is a sales coordinator at a cosmetics company. He meets up with the sales team to go over the annual sales figures. After two hours, the team members don't seem to be enthusiastic or paying attention at all.

B

Craig is interviewing for an IT specialist position. He is a strong candidate with over 20 years of experience. However, during the interview, the IT manager seems angry, defensive, and judgmental of his ideas. By the end, Craig is sure he won't get the job.

C

Carlota works as a party planner. She is having some problems with a client who wants to organize a birthday party for his son. Carlota is worried because he is demanding things outside of the budget and contract, and the party is tomorrow.

D

Akira has recently started her first job as an app developer. Her manager asked her to present an idea she's been working on to the senior app developers on her team. Despite working hard to prepare, she is very nervous during the presentation.

E

Alma is an elementary school teacher. One of her students keeps distracting her classmates and refuses to do the writing activity she has been given despite being warned repeatedly. So, Alma is asserting her authority.

F

Jack is a freelance video editor. He has received a text message from a client who wants some major changes in the video he edited a while ago. He doesn't agree with the changes, and he's worried about making them now while he is busy with several other projects.

Scenario	Body Language	Message
A		
B		
C		
D		
E		
F		

B GROUPS Compare your answers with another pair.

Step 5 Project

A PAIRS **In your online course, you focused on your spontaneous facial expressions and gestures in reaction to others and how they are interpreted. Tell your partner about your findings. Read the example.**

I focused on my reactions, and I realized that I tend to roll my eyes when I think someone is exaggerating or rambling. I asked my sister about it, and she told me that it often discourages her from continuing a conversation with me. She said my eye-rolling makes her feel like she's being judged or that she doesn't have something valuable to say. I'm going to pay closer attention to this habit, so I don't seem like a disrespectful listener.

B SHARE **Discuss your list with the class.**

Step 6 Talk!

PAIRS **Body language is as much a part of our culture as our verbal language. How we send and receive messages through our body language is very much influenced by our culture. Even the most common gestures can mean different things in different cultures. Look at the chart below and discuss the questions.**

Gesture		Meaning / Countries
Shaking head from side-to-side		**No:** Countries throughout North, South, and Central America, Europe, Asia, and the Middle East
		Yes: Albania and Bulgaria
Curling the index finger toward the palm of the hand	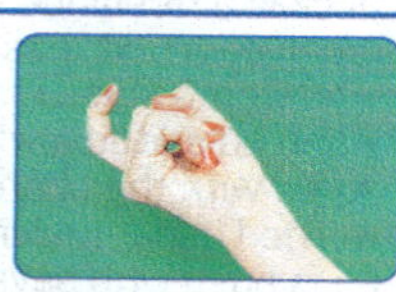	**Come here:** US, various English-speaking countries
		The dog call (*rude to be used to summon people*)**:** Philippines, Korea, and parts of Latin America
		Death: Singapore
Making eye contact		**Sign of respect and interest:** Western Europe, US
		Sign of disrespect (*between unfamiliar people, or those of different genders or social classes*)**:** Hispanic, Asian, Middle Eastern, and Native American cultures

- What do the gestures above mean to you?
- Which meanings surprised you the most?
- What are some common gestures used in your culture or country? Do you know if these gestures are universal?

Step 7 Going forward

A PAIRS **In your online course, you reflected on how you could improve your non-communication skills after studying more about nonverbal communication. Discuss. Listen to the example.**

B SHARE **Present your ideas to the class.**

VOCABULARY PRACTICE
Go to page 74.

I can explain how to use and interpret nonverbal communication professionally. ☐

2

MODULE

Communication 2

Persuasive Communication

DISCUSSION STRATEGIES

Go to page 68.

Step 1 Get started

A Refresh your memory! Watch the *What You'll Learn* video.

B Look at the photo. Which persuasive communication strategies is the woman using to persuade her teammates? What else can she do to be more persuasive?

C Check your understanding. Go to page 55.

Step 2 Tell your story

A THINK **In your online course, you thought about a time when you had to persuade someone to do what you wanted them to do. Did you manage to persuade them? If so, how? If not, why? Listen to the example.**

B PAIRS **Discuss your story.**

C SHARE **Tell your story to the class.**

Step 3 Take away

A PAIRS **Use your notes from the online module and match the words with the correct definitions or examples.**

Cialdini's principles	
_____ **1.** Reciprocity	**a.** While buying yourself a cup of coffee, you bring one to your colleague with sugar and extra milk – just the way she likes it.
_____ **2.** Authority	**b.** You send a birthday card to a friend who sent one to you on your previous birthday.
_____ **3.** Liking someone	**c.** You buy a particular brand of toothpaste because your dentist recommended it.

Aristotle's tools	
_____ **4.** Logos	**a.** This is an appeal to someone's sense of credibility. It involves the knowledge and expertise of the speaker.
_____ **5.** Ethos	**b.** This is an appeal to someone's emotional state. It involves the use of feelings and emotions.
_____ **6.** Pathos	**c.** This is an appeal to someone's sense of logic. It involves the use of statistics, facts, charts, and figures.

Other techniques	
_____ **7.** Funneling	**a.** This technique involves engaging an audience with an anecdote in order to get them to empathize with, agree with, or relate to the speaker.
_____ **8.** Storytelling	**b.** This technique involves starting with general questions, and then crafting more specific questions to arrive at a deeper understanding, motivation, or need.

B GROUPS **Compare your answers with another pair.**

Step 4 Activate your knowledge

A THINK Read and listen to the three speeches. Check the persuasive technique used or described in each one.

Scenario 1

As seen in this figure, there is a considerable decrease in the number of customers purchasing our wired earbuds. To increase our market share, we in the product development team believe we need to invest in wireless technology and improve our earbuds' design.

Which of Aristotle's tools of persuasion is utilized by Lisa?

- ☐ logos
- ☐ ethos
- ☐ pathos

Scenario 2

When I first started my online clothing store, sales were low and customers rarely returned. Then I started to give away a free gift with every purchase: a small necklace or leather bracelet with the buyer's initial on it. That helped me to build a base of loyal customers, many of whom leave very positive reviews on my website after their purchases. Their reviews have convinced more customers to buy from my store, and sales have doubled in six months.

Which of Cialdini's principles of persuasion is utilized by Lorenzo?

- ☐ authority
- ☐ reciprocity
- ☐ liking someone

Scenario 3

A few years ago, my husband and I were eating out while on vacation when he got food poisoning. While waiting in the hospital for my husband to be treated, I thought about all of the times on our travels that we ended up eating unappetizing meals in strange places after roaming the streets and scrolling down search results on our phones. After that trip, I started to work on an app that would save travelers from these kinds of problems, and guess what? We're no longer choosing what we eat by chance or wasting a lot of time to find a good place to eat. By using this free app, people can find places to eat delicious food all around the world without any hassle. Now I'd like you to help me bring this app to the next level.

Which persuasion technique is being used by Sarah?

- ☐ funneling and asking effective questions
- ☐ liking someone
- ☐ storytelling

B PAIRS Read and listen to the scenarios again. Discuss your answers to the questions.

1. How else can Lisa convince her employers to invest in wireless technology?
2. How else can Lorenzo increase his sales?
3. How else can Sarah convince investors to help her improve her app?

C SHARE Present your ideas to the class.

Step 5 Project

A PAIRS In your online course, you did online research to find another one of Cialdini's principles of persuasion. Explain what it is and why it is persuasive. Read the example.

I learned about Cialdini's principle of social proof. It's the idea that before we make decisions, we usually check what people around us are doing. Basically, social proof confirms that what we are about to do has been done before, which makes it feel safer. People are more likely to choose what's common or popular in their community than what isn't. This rings true for me. I feel much more confident buying something online when I see a bunch of positive customer reviews written about it.

B SHARE Discuss your findings with the class.

Step 6 Talk!

PAIRS Some researchers believe that storytelling is more persuasive than providing statistical information, while others claim the opposite. There is also a third group who assert that using facts and storytelling together is the best option. Read what each group of researchers has to say and then answer the questions.

What researchers who favor storytelling say:

- Facts and figures just inform people, but what makes them reach a decision is to build an emotional connection to an idea, which is more possible with storytelling.
- Storytelling is a way to communicate our unique experiences, and people are more likely to be convinced by the personal experiences of people they trust.

What researchers who favor data say:

- Stories are personal experiences, but statistics are objective facts, which are more trustworthy.
- Storytelling can only work if your facts are weak. However, if your facts are strong, it's more persuasive to present the facts only, without any stories that may dilute their truth.

What researchers who favor a combination say:

- Storytelling may be a great tool to get people to empathize with you on some level, but without facts it may not be enough to persuade them to change their opinions or take action.
- Stories give the statistical data a meaning.

- In your opinion, which is more persuasive: storytelling, statistics, or a combination of both? Why?
- Do you think that the topic has any effect on the persuasiveness of storytelling or statistical data? If so, how? For which topics is each approach most persuasive?

Step 7 Going forward

A PAIRS In your online course, you reflected on how you could develop your power of persuasion skills after studying more about persuasive communication. Discuss. Listen to the example.

B SHARE Present your ideas to the class.

VOCABULARY PRACTICE Go to page 75.

I can describe ways to develop my persuasive communication skills. ☐

3 MODULE

Goal Setting

Sticking to Your Goals

DISCUSSION STRATEGIES

Go to page 68.

Step 1 Get started

A Refresh your memory! Watch the *What You'll Learn* video.

B Look at the photo. How could it be related to sticking to goals? What do people need to do in order to stay committed to their goals?

C Check your understanding. Go to page 56.

Step 2 Tell your story

A THINK In your online course, you thought about a goal you set for your career or personal life. Which strategies did you use to stick to your goal? Listen to the example.

B PAIRS Discuss your story.

C SHARE Tell your story to the class.

Step 3 Take away

A PAIRS Use your notes from the online module and the words in the box to complete the chart with the list of dos and don'ts for setting and sticking to your goals.

patient goals reward support values develop put off
demands results expectations dedicate inspire

DOs	DON'Ts
• Choose goals that ____________ or excite you. • Set goals that align with your core ____________. • Stay ____________, consistent, and positive. • Set aside time to ____________ to your goal. • Get the tools, training, and ____________ you need. • ____________ yourself when you achieve a major step. • ____________ routines and habits.	• Don't base your goals on others' ____________. • Don't ____________ your tasks. Avoid procrastination. • Don't set too many ____________ for yourself at the same time. • Don't expect quick ____________. • Don't let the ____________ of other people distract you from your goals.

B GROUPS Compare your answers with another pair. Can you think of more DOs and DON'Ts?

Step 4 Activate your knowledge

A THINK Read the three scenarios about people setting goals. Then complete the chart.

SCENARIO 1 • GRACE

Grace works at a company which does a lot of business with Spanish-speaking customers. As the executive assistant, she sometimes needs to talk to and build connections with them. Her Spanish is not so good, but she liked learning Spanish when she was at school, and she wants to improve. So, she found a Spanish language school close to her office and enrolled in a course. She invited a colleague to attend with her, and now they both dedicate two evenings a week to taking Spanish classes.

SCENARIO 2 • LEVI

Levi is a professional artist. His work is on display at a local gallery, but he doesn't get paid unless his work is sold. He needs to earn money more regularly to pay his bills. Mike, a friend of Levi's, designs T-shirts for different clothing stores and seems to get paid well. Levi asked him for advice to get started in that business, too. Mike suggested that Levi spend at least an hour a day with him for about two weeks so that Mike can show him how he operates his whole business: choosing suppliers, using the printing equipment, selling to retailers, and running his online store. They met three times, but then Levi got very busy with the digital marketing course he's taking three days a week to learn how to promote his art on social media. He postponed again because he teaches art to a group of economically disadvantaged children, and he got busy with them. Then he had to attend events at the gallery and work on some new pieces of his own. He doesn't know when he'll be able to meet with Mike next.

SCENARIO 3 • NOVA

Nova is an animator working on the visual effects team at an advertising agency. She is quite creative and artistic, but she needs to improve some of her technical skills to keep up with the advancements in technology. She has to learn how to use software for 3D animation. To that end, she's been taking classes for about a month. She knows it's going to take several more months to learn the software because it's very complicated. However, she's very happy to be learning something new and improving her skills as an animator. She's promised herself a nice vacation once she's produced her first 3D animation.

	What was her/his goal?	Why did she/he want to achieve it?
Grace 		
Levi 		
Nova 		

B PAIRS **Read the scenarios again. Did they stay committed to their goals? If yes, how? If not, why not? Discuss.**

C GROUPS **Compare your answers with another pair.**

Step 5 Project

A PAIRS In your online course, you focused on your professional and personal life goals and took notes on how you will stay committed. Present your goals and plans to your partner. Read the example.

I'm working as a lab technician, but my career goal is to become a full-time writer. To stay committed to this goal, I will work on freelance writing projects to help build up my portfolio. Instead of feeling demotivated by the feedback I receive on these projects, I will use it to focus on what I need to do to improve my writing skills. I'll look for and attend writing workshops near me and mark those dates on my calendar. I will spend time every evening reading books by writers who inspire me.

B SHARE Discuss your notes with the class.

Step 6 Talk!

PAIRS Look at the life goals people want to achieve. Then discuss the questions.

LIFE GOALS

1. Find purpose in life
2. Be healthy and fit
3. Have strong relationships
4. Have financial freedom
5. Have a meaningful career
6. Lead an adventurous life
7. Travel the world
8. Contribute to society

- Why do you think these are the most popular goals?
- Which ones would you choose for yourself? Why?
- Are there any others you would add? Which ones?

Step 7 Going forward

A PAIRS In your online course, you reflected on how you could improve your goal setting after studying more about sticking to goals. Discuss. Listen to the example.

B SHARE Present your ideas to the class.

VOCABULARY PRACTICE
Go to page 76.

I can describe specific strategies for staying committed to my goals. ☐

4

MODULE

Teamwork

Building Emotional Intelligence

DISCUSSION STRATEGIES
Go to page 68.

Step 1 Get started

A Refresh your memory! Watch the *What You'll Learn* video.

B Look at the photo. Do you think this team looks like an emotionally intelligent team? Why? What are the main characteristics of an emotionally intelligent team?

C Check your understanding. Go to page 57.

Step 2 Tell your story

A THINK **In your online course, you thought about a time when you were a member of a group or team. Was it an emotionally intelligent team? What made you think so? Listen to the example.**

B PAIRS **Discuss your story.**

C SHARE **Tell your story to the class.**

Step 3 Take away

A PAIRS **Discuss how emotional intelligence can affect teamwork. Complete the chart with the words in the box. There are two extra words.**

comfortable	emotions	employees	mistakes	motivate	respect	solve

In teams with emotional intelligence, members ...

feel welcome, ________________, and safe.

try to include new ________________ .

express their thoughts and ________________ each other's ideas.

try to learn from ________________ and failures.

take proactive solution-oriented steps to ________________ any problems.

B SHARE **Compare your ideas with another pair. Can you add more to the list?**

Step 4 Activate your knowledge

A PAIRS **Read the stories told by different people about their teamwork experiences. Then check the correct answers to the questions.**

STORY 1

Monica

Eve, Ian, and I were good friends in school. When we graduated, we decided to open a floral shop together because we all loved flowers. Ian had a business degree, Eve had a marketing degree, and I had a design degree, so we thought we had everything covered. Things were great at first, but soon Ian started complaining that Eve and I weren't business-minded enough and that we weren't managing the finances well. We had originally planned to share all the shop-keeping hours evenly, but Ian argued that since he had to do all the accounting work, he'd work fewer hours in the shop. But often he would tell us at the last minute that he wasn't coming in and we had to cover his hours. Plus, we all had families – and Eve and I seemed to have more household responsibilities than Ian – but he didn't seem to care about that. After a year and a half, we closed the shop.

Which components of EQ did Ian lack? Explain.

☐ Self-regulation ☐ Empathy ☐ Motivation ☐ Social skills

STORY 2

I have been working as a graphic designer for almost ten years now. Last year, my employer wanted our company to be involved in a project to raise awareness about autism. I was really excited about it. My sister's son is autistic, so I know how hard life can be for families dealing with autism. Anyway, I was asked to team up with the digital media marketing specialist, Matias, and the content developer, Yua. Together, the three of us had to come up with a creative idea. During our meetings, Matias and I suggested lots of things we could do, but Yua didn't seem to share our enthusiasm or interest. She usually stayed quiet. She said she didn't know anyone with autism and would rather be working on a different project. That hurt my feelings, given how passionate I am about the cause. Eventually, Yua stopped showing up to our meetings, and Matias and I completed most of the work.

Which components of EQ did Yua lack? Explain.

☐ **Self-regulation** ☐ **Empathy** ☐ **Motivation** ☐ **Social skills**

B PAIRS **Read Monica's and Darius's stories again. Discuss the strategies that could have been implemented to improve their team's EQ. Then complete the table.**

MONICA'S STORY		
Lacking EQ components	**How could Ian have been more emotionally intelligent?**	**How could the team have helped Ian improve his EQ?**

DARUIS' STORY		
Lacking EQ components	**How could Yua have been more emotionally intelligent?**	**How could the team have helped Yua improve her EQ?**

C SHARE **Present your ideas to the class. Take notes while others are presenting. Then vote on the best strategies for improving emotional intelligence in each story.**

Step 5 Project

A PAIRS In your online course, you created a survey focusing on the challenges people face when working on teams. Share your findings with a partner. Read the example.

According to the results of my survey, acknowledging team members' emotions is what challenges people most. I found out that people who have stressful, demanding jobs with tight schedules and lots of responsibility are more likely to fail to see the importance of empathy when working on a team. To address that challenge, the survey participants suggested ideas like inviting feedback at the end of every meeting, requesting that their company provide training on emotional intelligence to their teams, and leaving a feedback box in the office for people to share their feelings anonymously – and setting aside time to regularly review and respond to that feedback as a group.

B SHARE Discuss your findings with the class.

Step 6 Talk!

PAIRS More and more people are aware of emotional intelligence and its role in the workplace. Look at the infographic and discuss.

95% of HR managers and 99% of workers believe it's essential to have high emotional intelligence.

Nearly half of HR managers think teaching soft skills is harder than teaching technical ones.

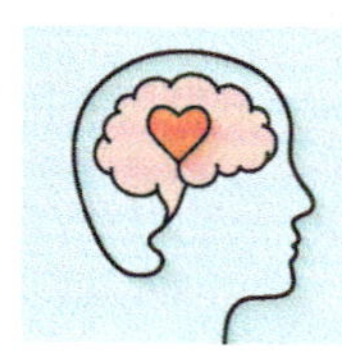

92% of workers believe that their emotional intelligence is high, but only 74% say the same about their managers.

Nearly 90% of workers link being able to control emotions with professionalism.

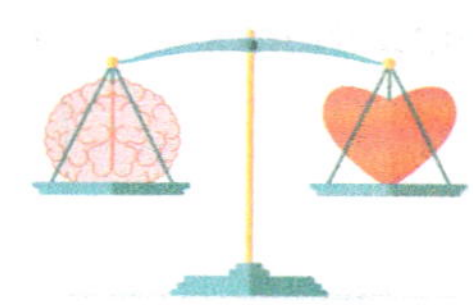

About 20% of employees say EQ is more important than IQ at work; 65% say it's as important.

Step 7 Going forward

A PAIRS In your online course, you reflected on how you could improve the emotional intelligence of a team or group that you are a member of after studying more about emotionally intelligent teams. Discuss. Listen to the example.

B SHARE Present your ideas to the class.

VOCABULARY PRACTICE
Go to page 77.

I can explain what emotionally intelligent teams look like and the benefits of them. ☐

5

MODULE

Critical Thinking

Decision Making

DISCUSSION STRATEGIES

Go to page 68.

Step 1 Get started

A Refresh your memory! Watch the *What You'll Learn* video.

B Look at the photo. The woman is trying to reach a decision. What advice would you give her about how to make the best decision?

C Check your understanding. Go to page 58.

Step 2 Tell your story

A THINK In your online course, you thought about a time when you made an important decision in your personal or professional life. What happened? Were you happy with your decision? Listen to the example.

B PAIRS Discuss your story.

C SHARE Tell your story to the class.

Step 3 Take away

A PAIRS Use your notes from the online module and fill in the blanks with the words in the box to complete the seven steps of decision-making process.

choose	decision	gather	identify	options	outcomes	review

1. ______________ the decision.
2. ______________ data.
3. Consider the ______________.
4. Evaluate possible ______________.
5. ______________ the best option.
6. Act on the ______________.
7. ______________ your decision.

B GROUPS Compare your answers with another pair.

Step 4 Activate your knowledge

A THINK **Read the two scenarios and write the steps of the decision-making process in Step 3 included in each one.**

Scenario 1

Haru works as a creative director at an ad agency. A client of theirs is trying to break into the market with a new soft drink. Haru and the creative department need to come up with a campaign slogan for the product. So, he asks the two copywriters on the team to research the slogans other soft drink producers use and to have interviews with the client to learn more about the product and what makes it unique. In the meantime, the other members of the creative team gather a focus group to taste the drink and get their feedback on it. Then the creative department comes together to share their information and present possible slogans. Among those slogans, Haru chooses the one he likes best and asks the designers to work on the art and design based on this slogan.

Scenario 2

Enola and Ross are opening a coffee shop together. They need to buy a commercial espresso machine for the shop. They know a man, Jamie, who's retiring from the business. Jamie offers to sell them his espresso machine for a very cheap price. Enola and Ross quickly accept the offer, excited not to have to buy a new, expensive machine. At the grand opening of Enola and Ross's coffee shop, the espresso machine breaks after serving just ten customers. Having had that unfortunate incident on such an important day, Enola and Ross agree that they need to research future purchases more carefully.

Steps in the decision-making process	
Haru	______________________ ______________________ ______________________ ______________________
Enola and Ross	______________________ ______________________ ______________________ ______________________

B PAIRS **What could they do to improve the decision-making process? Discuss and take notes.**

Haru: ______________________

____

Enola and Ross: ______________________

____

C SHARE **Present your ideas to the class.**

Step 5 Project

A PAIRS In your online course, you described how you will apply the seven steps in the decision-making process to a future decision. Tell your partner about it. Read the example.

I've been thinking of doing something fun and beneficial for myself, like joining a gym. After identifying the decision I need to make (which gym I should attend), I can gather data. First, I can ask my friends if they are happy with their gyms. I can also look online for other gyms near my home or work and read reviews about them. I can investigate which ones offer spin and yoga classes, which I'm most interested in, and I can compare prices. Next, I can visit the best options. Then I can evaluate the possible outcomes of going to each gym given my schedule, workout goals, and budget. After that, I can choose a gym and join it. Finally, once I've been going there for a while, I can review my decision and either renew or cancel my membership.

B SHARE Discuss your ideas with the class.

Step 6 Talk!

PAIRS Research shows that as we overthink our decisions, our stress level increases. As a result, our happiness, creativity, and productivity decrease. Read the posts below and discuss the questions.

For my literature class, I need to write a reflection on a book in two weeks. First, I need to choose the book from a list of ten that the professor gave us. I spent almost a week thinking about how to choose the book. I wondered if I should read all of them, but I knew that would take too long. I thought about reading the shortest one, but I didn't like the first chapter and gave up on that one. The others were about the same length and all available at my library. How should I choose between them? I read the summaries on the back of the books, but they didn't say much. I tried reading a little about the authors, but that didn't help either. So maybe I really do need to start reading them all to help me decide...

I'm a senior marketing executive for an e-commerce website that sells home decor. Recently, I came up with an idea about how to increase our sales: App-Deco! It would work like this. A customer would see an item in the real world that they like, for example, a beautiful vase in a coffee shop. They take a picture of it through the app, which then recommends very similar items on our website. When I presented my idea to the team, they loved it! But then everyone had different ideas about how to proceed. Joe thought we should immediately hire an expert in app development to work on it. Alexa, on the other hand, saw the potential in selling the idea to another company. Phyllis, liking the idea but worried about the cost, said that we should try to get the producers of the best-selling items on our website to invest in it. These are just three of a dozen of ideas from the team, which we debated over the course of six weeks. No action was taken, and now people have stopped bringing up the idea all together.

1. What problems are these two people having? What can you suggest to help them resolve their issues?
2. Have you ever gotten stuck in the decision-making process and been unable to decide something for yourself? What was it? What happened?
3. Have you ever been a part of a group (at home or at work) that had a great idea but could never agree on how to make it happen? What was the idea? Why couldn't you execute it?

Step 7 Going forward

A PAIRS In your online course, you reflected on how you could improve you decision-making skills after studying more about the decision-making processes. Discuss. Listen to the example.

B SHARE Present your ideas to the class.

VOCABULARY PRACTICE
Go to page 78.

I can explain the seven steps to effective decision making. ☐

6 MODULE

Leadership

Leadership Styles

DISCUSSION STRATEGIES

Go to page 68.

Step 1 Get started

A Refresh your memory! Watch the *What You'll Learn* video.

B Look at the photo. Which leadership style do you think it represents? Why do you think so? What do you think is the best leadership style?

C Check your understanding. Go to page 59.

Step 2 Tell your story

A THINK In your online course, you thought about a time that you worked with a leader at work, at school, or in your personal life. Which leadership style did the leader demonstrate? Listen to the example.

B PAIRS Discuss your story.

C SHARE Tell your story to the class.

Step 3 Take away

A PAIRS Review your notes from the online module and match each leadership style to the correct description.

LEADERSHIP STYLES	
____ 1. Autocratic	a. can lead to high staff turnover as workers often find few opportunities to develop, but as the expectations and the rewards are clear, short-term goals can be achieved quicker
____ 2. Participative	b. involves asking employees' opinions and input, which boosts team spirit but can be a slow and time-consuming process
____ 3. Delegative	c. is most effective when a team needs to undergo major changes or improvements, but may lead to a poor work-life balance or burnout
____ 4. Transformational	d. works best with a highly experienced team, providing them opportunities for growth, but is likely to fail if inexperienced members are not given enough guidance or mentoring
____ 5. Transactional	e. may work in crisis or extreme situations where quick and essential decisions are required, but may create an atmosphere where employees don't feel safe expressing their opinions as they are expected to follow the orders

B SHARE Check your answers with the class.

Step 4 Activate your knowledge

A PAIRS Read the scenarios at five different companies [A-E]. Discuss which leadership style would be most effective at dealing with each scenario. Then complete the chart.

Company A

This company is downsizing, and a lot of people have been fired. The morale of the remaining workers is very low.

Company B

This company is getting ready to release a new product, and there's a big sales push. They want the sales force to capitalize on its release and sell it aggressively.

Company C

This company wants to be more involved in social responsibility projects. They'd like input from their staff about what they should do.

Company D

This company relies on technology to perform its daily functions. They are in a technological crisis because of a cyberattack. They need to take some immediate actions.

Company E

This company has highly experienced staff who are really good at handling their day-to-day jobs. They are up for new challenges and opportunities for growth.

Company	Which leadership style would be most effective in this situation?	Why?
A		
B		
C		
D		
E		

B GROUPS Join another pair and compare your answers.

C GROUPS Which leadership style would be the least effective in each situation? Discuss.

Step 5 Project

A PAIRS In your online course, you interviewed a person to learn more about their leadership style. Tell your partner about it. Read the example.

I interviewed a friend of mine who is a director of operations. She seems to have a combination of two dominant leadership styles. She uses an autocratic approach when she's handling conflicts. She gives direct orders to help solve the problem. At other times, she uses a delegative approach. She assigns tasks to experienced team members and gives them the independence to handle the tasks in their own way.

B SHARE Discuss your findings with the class.

Step 6 Talk!

PAIRS Successful people develop different leadership styles based on their values, personality, experience, and the needs of their organization. Read some famous leaders' quotes and discuss the questions.

"*To me, leadership is not about necessarily being the loudest in the room, but instead being the bridge, or the thing that is missing in the discussion and trying to build a consensus from there.*"
— **Jacinda Ardern**, the 40th prime minister of New Zealand and the leader of the Labour Party

"*My job is not to be easy on people. My job is to make them better.*"
— **Steve Jobs**, the chairman, chief executive officer (CEO), and co-founder of Apple Inc.

"*Integrity, insight, and inclusiveness are the three essential qualities of leadership.*"
— **Sadhguru Sadhguru**, Indian yoga guru

- What do you think are the dominant leadership styles of these leaders?
- Do you agree or disagree with their ideas about leadership? Explain.
- Based on their quotes, how do you think people working with these leaders describe them?
- Can you name any other famous leaders and guess their leadership styles?

Step 7 Going forward

A PAIRS In your online course, you reflected on how you could develop your leadership style after studying more about the leadership styles. Discuss. Listen to the example.

B SHARE Present your ideas to the class.

VOCABULARY PRACTICE
Go to page 79.

I can describe the five common leadership styles. ☐

7

MODULE

Self-Management

The Power of Deadlines

DISCUSSION STRATEGIES

Go to page 68.

Step 1 Get started

A Refresh your memory! Watch the *What You'll Learn* video.

B Look at the photo. The man is feeling stressed. What advice would you give him about how to set efficient deadlines?

C Check your understanding. Go to page 60.

Step 2 Tell your story

A THINK In your online course, you thought about a time when you missed a deadline in your personal or professional life. What was the deadline and why you were not able to meet it? Listen to the example.

B PAIRS Discuss your story.

C SHARE Tell your story to the class.

Step 3 Take away

A PAIRS Use your notes from the online module and fill in the blanks with the words in the box.

attention calendar complex fixed motivate procrastination productive realistic self-imposed

DEADLINES	
Types:	soft = flexible, 1 ______________ hard = 2 ______________, set by others
Benefits:	get us to complete tasks and projects focus our 3 ______________ 4 ______________ us stop 5 ______________ help us to become more 6 ______________ and perform better
Strategies:	Plan carefully. Break down 7 ______________ tasks. Assign a 8 ______________ amount of time for each part. Put time slots in your 9 ______________.

B GROUPS Compare your answers with another pair.

Step 4 Activate your knowledge

A PAIRS Read the two scenarios and check the strategies they used to set and meet deadlines.

SCENARIO 1

Nova is a freelance editor working on a new course book for a publishing company. He's working with an editorial assistant and three different authors. The publishing company gave Nova a deadline for the submission of the final drafts. He asked the editorial assistant to plan interim deadlines for three drafts of each unit of the course book, setting the final submission date one week before the publisher's deadline to allow for possible delays. He also asked the editorial assistant to set reminders for each interim due date in their shared calendar. The authors began writing immediately, but it quickly became clear that they would need more time on the first drafts than planned. So, the schedule was updated to make the first draft phase longer and the others shorter. However, by the second draft, the authors were still struggling to meet the interim deadlines. Nova notified the publishing company to see if the final deadline could be postponed.

SCENARIO 2

Lauren is a psychologist with over 10 years of experience. She sees at least two clients a day and writes a weekly post on her psychology blog. She's also recently started a specialized training course. To complete the first module of the course, she has to submit an assignment in six weeks. She believes it will take four full days to complete the assignment. She's very busy over the next four weeks, but she sets reminders on her phone to work on the assignment for four days after that. She has always tracked her time while writing her blog posts, and she knows it usually takes her almost five hours to write each one. So, she plans to skip posting to her blog during those two weeks. After the first day of working on the assignment, Lauren realizes that she will need more than four days to complete it, and she's wondering how she'll find the time to get it done.

Strategies for maintaining deadlines	Nova	Lauren
Break down the task into smaller parts	☐	☐
Assign a realistic amount of time to each part	☐	☐
Add some extra time to the schedule	☐	☐
Set reminders	☐	☐
Start working right away	☐	☐
Track time	☐	☐
Revise the schedule when necessary	☐	☐
Ask for an extension at an early stage	☐	☐
Eliminate non-essential tasks	☐	☐

B PAIRS Choose one of the scenarios and discuss what other strategies for setting and meeting deadlines could have been used.

C SHARE Present your ideas to the class. Vote for the best suggestions for each scenario.

Step 5 Project

A PAIRS In your online course, you set a deadline for a task and noted down your plan to meet the deadline. Tell your partner about it. Read the example.

Improving my French has been on my checklist for a long time, but I've never managed to dedicate time to it. Whenever I thought about signing up for an online course, something popped up and I backed out. So, I decided to start with brushing up on my listening skills first. I've found an app and I'm thinking of using it while commuting because all I need is my phone and headphones. The app also sends reminders and shows my progress, which will definitely motivate me. After having completed the listening modules, I'll plan how to improve my speaking skills next.

B SHARE Discuss your list with the class.

Step 6 Talk!

PAIRS Read each person's problem with deadlines. Then discuss setting and meeting deadlines. Use the questions below to help guide your conversation.

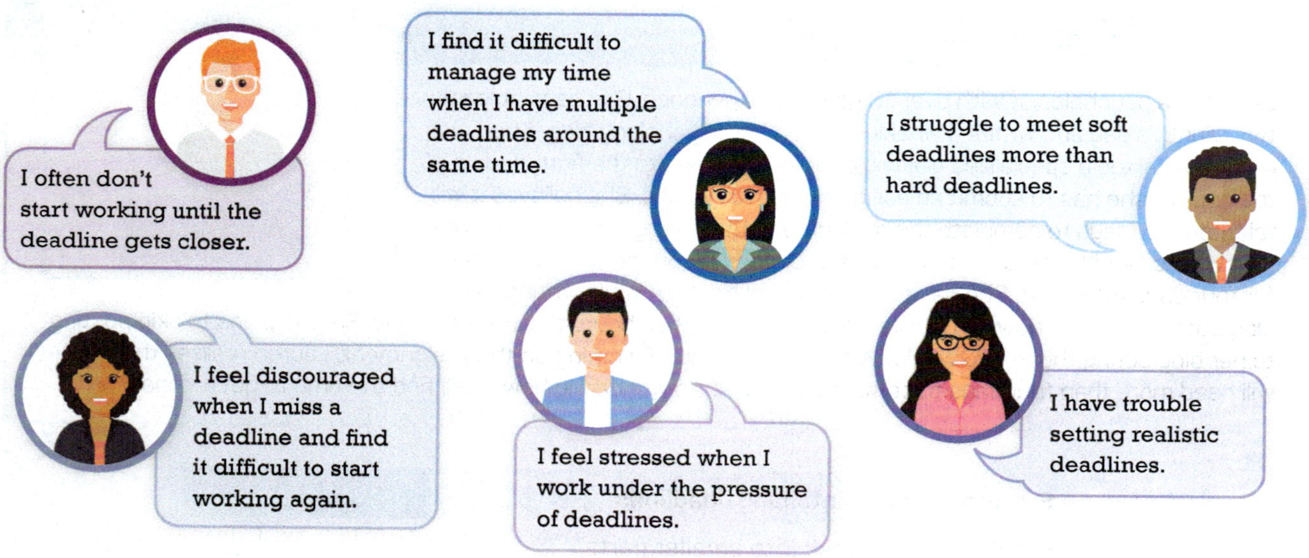

- Which of these problems do you have with setting and meeting deadlines? Why?
- What can you do to overcome these problems?

Step 7 Going forward

A PAIRS In your online course, you reflected on how you could set and meet deadlines after studying more about the power of deadlines. Discuss. Listen to the example.

B SHARE Present your ideas to the class.

VOCABULARY PRACTICE
Go to page 80.

I can describe ways to set and meet deadlines successfully. ☐

8

MODULE

Wellness

Work-Life Balance

DISCUSSION STRATEGIES

Go to page 68.

Step 1 Get started

A Refresh your memory! Watch the *What You'll Learn* video.

B Look at the photo. The woman is working overtime. What would you suggest she do to improve her work-life balance?

C Check your understanding. Go to page 61.

Step 2 Tell your story

A THINK In your online course, you thought about a time when you noticed an imbalance between your work and home lives. How did the imbalance affect your physical and/or mental well-being? Listen to the example.

B PAIRS Discuss your story.

C SHARE Tell your story to the class.

Step 3 Take away

A PAIRS Review your notes from the online module and match the sentences.

_____ **1.** Lack of work-life balance can affect our mental health by	**a.** when we choose tasks that interfere with each other.
_____ **2.** In order to stay physically healthy and well,	**b.** we do not recharge our batteries.
_____ **3.** Our productivity decreases when	**c.** we need to review our to-do list.
_____ **4.** We need to be flexible	**d.** leading to stress, depression, and burnout.
_____ **5.** Sometimes, to ease the burden of everyday tasks,	**e.** to meet the everyday challenges and demands of our jobs
_____ **6.** Multitasking may result in failure when	**f.** we need enough time to exercise and sleep.

B SHARE Check your answers with the class.

Step 4 Activate your knowledge

A PAIRS Karl, James, and Luna are employees at the same company. Each is going to meet confidentially with a wellness coach hired by the company. Before the meeting, they were asked to fill out a form about their work-life balance. Read and listen to their forms and take notes in the chart about each employee's problem.

FORM 1

Karl

How would you describe your work-life balance?

Until two years ago, when we used to work in the office, I would say I had a good work-life balance. I could shift my attention away from work when I got home. I used to feel happier and more willing to work. But, since we started working from home, I feel like I am working 24/7. Work has become my whole life. My energy level is almost always low, and I feel like I have forgotten how to have fun.

FORM 2

James

How would you describe your work-life balance?

Recently, my work-life balance has not been great. I have been promoted to a leadership position in my department. I used to be an educational consultant, but now I am responsible for managing a team of consultants. The problem is that until the company hires someone to do my old job, I have to continue doing it while also taking on my new responsibilities. It's overwhelming. I feel like I'm always bouncing back and forth between different tasks and hardly getting anything done. I have trouble prioritizing my to-do list because everything seems to require my immediate attention. I end up working at home at night and even on weekends instead of spending time with my family.

FORM 3

Luna

How would you describe your work-life balance?

I have noticed some imbalances between my work and private life lately. As a customer services specialist, I help our customers solve problems with the digital products they use. The faster the problems are solved, the happier our customers are, and therefore, the more successful I am at work. I started to work here almost a year ago. At first, I was so happy to have a desk job and be able to help resolve people's issues with our products and services, but I now feel burned out. Because I try to be constantly available for customers during my shift, I hardly take breaks. I barely know my colleagues since I have no time to chat with them except for our lunch breaks.

	Problems with work-life balance	Suggestions
Karl		
James		
Luna		

B PAIRS **If you were the wellness coach, what suggestions would you make to improve each person's work-life balance? Add your ideas to the chart.**

C SHARE **Compare your suggestions with another pair.**

Step 5 Project

A PAIRS In your online course, you searched and created a list of additional tips for achieving work-life balance. Share the tips you think are the most useful with your partner. Read the example.

While I was searching for tips on achieving work-life balance, I came across an article that focused on the importance of saying no. It suggests getting clear with yourself about what's essential and what's not – and saying yes only to what really matters to you. It's said that often we do things because we think we should, not because we really want to or need to. I think it's a useful tip, because once we start saying no to unnecessary or undesirable things, we get more focused on the important things we say yes to.

B SHARE Discuss your list with the class.

Step 6 Talk!

PAIRS According to the Organization for Economic Co-operation and Development (OECD) these are the countries with the best work-life balance. Look at the *Did you know ...?* and discuss the questions.

Top 5 Countries with the Best Work-Life Balance:

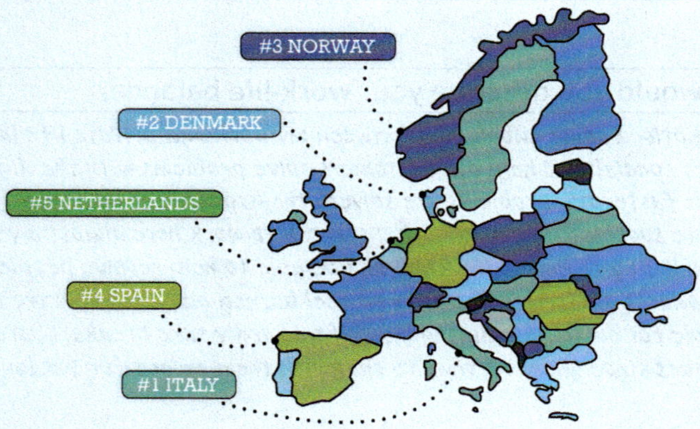

Did you know...?

In Italy, full-time workers allocate almost 70% of their time in a day to personal care and leisure.

In Denmark and in Norway, only around 1% of employees work more than 40 hours in a week, while it is 2% in Spain and 0% in Netherlands.

- Which factors do you think the OECD considers when determining the order of countries on this list?
- What do you know about these five countries? Are you surprised to see them at the top of the list?
- How much time do you spend for your personal care and leisure in a day? Is it sufficient or not? If not, what can you do about it?

Step 7 Going forward

A PAIRS In your online course, you reflected on how you could improve your work-life balance after studying more about it. Discuss. Listen to the example.

B SHARE Present your ideas to the class.

VOCABULARY PRACTICE Go to page 81.

I can describe ways to maintain work-life balance. ☐

9

MODULE

Social Responsibility

Ethical Decisions

DISCUSSION STRATEGIES

Go to page 68.

Step 1 Get started

A Refresh your memory! Watch the *What You'll Learn* video.

B Look at the photo. How can companies deal with ethical dilemmas?

C Check your understanding. Go to page 62.

Step 2 Tell your story

A THINK **In your online course, you thought about a time when you had an ethical dilemma in your personal or professional life. What was it and what did you do? Listen to the example.**

B PAIRS **Discuss your story.**

C SHARE **Tell your story to the class.**

Step 3 Take away

PAIRS **Review your notes from the online module and match the steps of the PLUS model for ethical decision making with the relevant questions.**

____ **1. P = Policies**	**a.** Does it satisfy my personal definition of right, good, and fair?
____ **2. L = Legal**	**b.** Does it conform to the universal principles and values that my organization has adopted?
____ **3. U = Universal**	**c.** Is it acceptable under the applicable laws and regulations?
____ **4. S = Self**	**d.** Is it consistent with my organization's codes of conduct, procedures, and guidelines?

Step 4 Activate your knowledge

A PAIRS **Read two common standards of professional conduct. Then apply the standards to the three scenarios below. Complete the chart.**

Standards of Professional Conduct

I. Preservation of Clients' Confidentiality
Information about current, former, and prospective clients must be kept confidential unless:
a. the information concerns illegal activities on the part of the client,
b. disclosure is required by law, or
c. the client permits disclosure of the information.

II. Loyalty to Employers
In matters related to their employment, employees must act for the benefit of their employer and not share confidential information, or otherwise cause harm to their employer.

SCENARIO 1

Jerry works at an international publishing company that has recently updated their product prices for the new sales season. A friend of his works for another publishing company, and they are in the process of updating their prices, too. While they were talking one day, Jerry's friend was complaining about how some of the managers wanted to raise prices too much. Knowing that the price changes for his company's products would be announced online soon, Jerry commented that the price increases didn't sound like too much to him. He admitted that they were about the same percentage that his company used to mark up their prices.

SCENARIO 2

Elaine works as an executive assistant for an IT company which is in the process of merging with another IT service provider. Her boss was engaging in private negotiations about the merger. While taking notes during one of those meetings, Elaine learned that once the two companies joined, many jobs would become redundant at her company, and some of her colleagues would be fired – including one of her close friends. She wanted to let her friend know about the situation so that she could begin looking for another job right away, but she was not allowed to discuss any of details about negotiation, or the deal could fall through. She kept the information to herself.

SCENARIO 3

Will works as an investment officer. One of his clients has been considering a donation of $30,000 to a charity. During a social gathering, Will meets Rachel who works at a charity organization for orphans. Rachel mentions her charity's urgent need for donors. In an effort to help, Will gives Rachel his client's name, phone number, and email address so she can contact him and ask for a donation.

	Related Code of Conduct	Ethical or unethical?
Jerry		
Elaine		
Will		

B GROUPS **Work with another pair and compare your answers. Discuss what you would have done differently and why.**

C GROUPS **Now that you've evaluated the decisions according to the P (policies and procedures) of the PLUS model, discuss how the other categories could be applied to make more ethical decisions: L (legal), U (universal values), and S (self).**

Step 5 Project

A PAIRS In your online course, you applied the PLUS model to an ethical dilemma at your workplace. Share it with your partner. Read the example.

In the past, I had colleagues who took more breaks than we were supposed to. It always bothered me because I ended up having to do more work than them. If I were to apply the PLUS model to this situation in the future, I would confirm the details of the company's policy about taking breaks and see what the consequences of breaking the rules were. I would either ask directly or observe how the other employees felt and reacted to this situation to find out if it aligns with the culture of the company or not. Finally, I would talk to my colleagues and share my concern because their behavior affects me. If nothing changed after that, I would report their behavior.

B SHARE Discuss your findings with the class.

Step 6 Talk!

PAIRS Read the facts about how employees and companies feel about ethical standards. Then discuss the questions.

82% of employees say that they would rather work for a company with high ethical standards and be paid less than work for a company with low ethical standards and be paid more.

36% of employees have quit their job because the company they worked for was unethical.

49% of companies care deeply about behaving ethically and work hard to develop user-friendly, employee-focused compliance programs.

94% of employees say that their company's ethics are important to them.

- How much does it matter to you if you work for a company with high ethical standards?
- Would you be willing to accept a lower salary to work for a highly ethical company? Why?
- Would you ever quit your job if you observed unethical behavior? Why?
- Have you ever worked for a company with a compliance program? If so, was it helpful?

Step 7 Going forward

A PAIRS In your online course, you reflected on how you could improve ethical decision-making skills after studying more about ethical decisions. Discuss. Listen to the example.

B SHARE Present your ideas to the class.

VOCABULARY PRACTICE
Go to page 82.

I can explain how to create an ethically strong workplace. ☐

10
MODULE

Branding

The Elevator Pitch

DISCUSSION STRATEGIES

Go to page 68.

Step 1 Get started

A Refresh your memory! Watch the *What You'll Learn* video.

B Look at the photo. How do you think the elevator pitch in the photo went? Why do you think so?

C Check your understanding. Go to page 63.

Step 2 Tell your story

A THINK In your online course, you thought about a time you used an elevator pitch or a time you wish you had. How did it go? Have you ever missed an opportunity to sell yourself or your idea to someone? Listen to the example.

B PAIRS Discuss your story.

C SHARE Tell your story to the class.

Step 3 Take away

A PAIRS Review your notes from the online module and fill in the blanks with the words in the box.

authentic	employers	goals	recruitment	seconds	words

Elevator pitch: a short, persuasive speech about you and your goals for potential [1]__________

- Length: 30-60 [2]__________ / 70-140 [3]__________
- Where to use? networking events, professional conferences, job or [4]__________ fairs.
- Benefits: clarifies your [5]__________; ensures you come across confident, sincere, and [6]__________

B PAIRS Put the main parts of an elevator pitch in order from 1 to 5.

_____ What you want to happen next
_____ Your relevant skills and experience
_____ What you do
_____ Who you are
_____ What job you want / What you want to achieve

Step 4 Activate your knowledge

A PAIRS Read and listen to the two elevator pitches prepared by Sara and Chris. Then complete the charts.

Scenario 1

Sara
- startup business owner
- looking for clients
- at a networking event

Three years ago, I started ALGOSALES where we develop personalized online sales funnels. That is, we design systems that guide potential customers along their online journeys toward making a purchase. Our mission is to provide automated solutions for companies selling their products online that will boost their sales. We started this business with the notion that online customers prefer an impeccable user experience tailored to their interests and needs. Therefore, we developed algorithms based on the four main stages a customer goes through before buying something: awareness, interest, decision, and action. Would you be interested in scheduling a follow-up meeting to talk about how we can help increase your sales revenue? Here's my business card.

What makes it effective?	What needs improving?

Scenario 2

Chris
- cook
- looking for a full-time position abroad
- at a job fair

After completing Culinary Arts School in the U.S. two years ago, I traveled to Europe and worked as a cook in restaurants in both Spain and France. There, I not only gained experience working under highly regarded chefs in professional kitchens, but I also learned so much about both Spanish and French cuisine and culture. For the next step of my career, I'm looking for a similar opportunity to explore the cuisine and cultures of the Far East – and I see that you have openings for cooks at your hotels in China, Thailand, and Japan. There are many Chinese, Thai, and Japanese restaurants here, but I don't think working in any of them would help me learn what I really want to. I believe learning a country's cuisine is easier when you live there because you are immersed in the culture and can interact with the people. So, I really want to work abroad. With my strong communication skills and ease at adapting to different cultures – as well as my interest in learning new languages – I think I would be a great cook at one of your hotels in Asia.

What makes it effective?	What needs improving?

B PAIRS **Choose an elevator pitch each. Rewrite it to make it more effective. Ask your partner for ideas and feedback as you revise.**

____

____

____

____

____

C PAIRS **Work with another partner. Deliver your revised pitches.**

Step 5 Project

A PAIRS In your online course, you created an elevator pitch. Share it with your partner. Read the example.

Hi, I'm Sandy. It's great to meet you. I work as a freelance marketing consultant, specializing in marketing campaigns and digital advertising. I currently serve several clients in the technology industry who I help reach new customers, keep existing ones, and increase their revenue. I'd love the opportunity to discuss how I can help you grow your client base, too. Would it be possible to setup a call next week to explore opportunities for us to work together?

B SHARE Share your elevator pitch with the class.

Step 6 Talk!

PAIRS Read about some of the most common mistakes people make when delivering an elevator pitch. Then discuss the questions.

1. Your pitch is too long.
2. You pack too much information in and lose your focus.
3. You use too many technical terms, which makes your pitch difficult to follow.
4. You talk too much about yourself rather than focusing on how you can help them.
5. You talk too fast, ramble, or sound hopeless.
6. You move back and forth or use your hands too much while talking.
7. You forget to ask for a follow-up conversation.

- Have you ever made or observed these mistakes in elevator pitches?
- Which ones do you think you are most likely to make in the future?
- How can you fix or prevent these mistakes?

Step 7 Going forward

A PAIRS In your online course, you reflected on how you could improve your elevator pitch after studying more about it. Discuss. Listen to the example.

B SHARE Present your ideas to the class.

VOCABULARY PRACTICE Go to page 83.

I can explain how to create a successful elevator pitch. ☐

11 MODULE

Job Search

Using Social Media

DISCUSSION STRATEGIES

Go to page 68.

Step 1 Get started

A Refresh your memory! Watch the *What You'll Learn* video.

B Look at the photo. What would you advise to the job seekers about how to search jobs by using social media?

C Check your understanding. Go to page 64.

Step 2 Tell your story

A THINK In your online course, you thought about a time when social media led to a job opportunity for you or someone you know. How did social media lead to this opportunity? Listen to the example.

B PAIRS Discuss your story.

C SHARE Tell your story to the class.

Step 3 Take away

A PAIRS Review your notes from the online module and fill in the blanks with the words in the box.

click	delete	endorsements	filter	network	overview	photo
positions	references	request	revise	update	up to date	

LinkedIn®: A social media platform used by individuals, executives, and organizations.	
What for?	• Search and apply for open [1] ______________ • Build your own professional [2] ______________ • Stay [3] ______________ with different businesses or organizations.
How to use?	• [4] ______________ on a button or tab that says *Jobs*. • Type in key words to see what's available. • [5] ______________ your search (e.g., by location, company, etc.) • Apply through the site.
Main parts of your profile	• Your photo • Summary: a brief [6] ______________ of your professional life and objectives • Skills along with [7] ______________ • Recommendations: written [8] ______________ from people in your network
Tips	• [9] ______________ your profile every 3 to 4 months. • Make sure your [10] ______________ still looks like you! • [11] ______________ your summary based on your current professional objectives. • Add new experiences and skills; [12] ______________ or reorder old ones. • Write and [13] ______________ new recommendations.

B SHARE Check your answers with the class.

Step 4 Activate your knowledge

A PAIRS Examine Kerry's LinkedIn profile and take notes about the strengths and weaknesses in terms of Photo, Summary, Skills and Recommendations.

Kerry Spencer

Interior Designer at Crown Plus
New York, United States
500+ connections

About

Being an interior designer is not simply about decorating a space. It's about telling people's stories. If you have a story to tell, I'll help you tell it by using a creative blend of architectural elements, fabrics, furniture, and other items important to you.

Each and every day, I get excited about new opportunities for collaboration and for making visions come to life. I do this by asking effective questions, listening carefully, and remaining open to new ideas. I also stay up to date with the latest trends by continually studying about new materials, techniques, and other developments in the field—all in an effort to offer the ideal solutions to my clients.

Most importantly, though, I believe in building trust through effective communication. It is the key to telling that story of yours.

Skills

Business development	Theater and Drama	Project management	Persuasion
Financial Analysis	Cultural Adaptation	Emotional Intelligence	Active listening

Creativity · **53** **Hannah Koskinen and 52 connections** have given endorsements for this skill.
Collaboration · **53** **Hannah Koskinen and 52 connections** have given endorsements for this skill.
AutoCAD · **25** **Aaron Kempton and 24 connections** have given endorsements for this skill.

Recommendations

Received (1) **Given (12)**

Andres Spencer
Client Insight Specialist at GLC
December 12, 2021

Kerry is extremely capable and always goes beyond her duties to get a job done. As her brother, I always see how hard she works to provide invaluable support to everyone around her.

B GROUPS Join another pair and compare your answers. Then discuss how Kerry could make her profile more attractive.

C SHARE Present your ideas to the class. Then discuss whether or not you'd be likely to hire Kerry for her services based on her profile.

Step 5 Project

A PAIRS **In your online course, you searched for jobs on LinkedIn. Describe the one that sounded the most appealing to you and explain why. Read the example.**

I found a job opening on LinkedIn for a financial specialist at a bank about 20 minutes from my home. The job interested me because I'm studying finance right now, and I hope to work in the financial industry one day. The qualifications are a degree in finance or a related field, experience in customer service, and strong communication and teamwork skills. The job responsibilities include helping customers by answering their calls and directing them toward the right financial solutions for their needs. The salary is very good, at $80,000 per year. I want to build up my qualifications so I can apply for similar jobs after I graduate.

B SHARE **Discuss your findings with the class.**

Step 6 Talk!

PAIRS **Research shows that more and more employers use various social media platforms to find suitable candidates. Look at the information below and answer the questions.**

Recruiters use different social media platforms to find candidates:

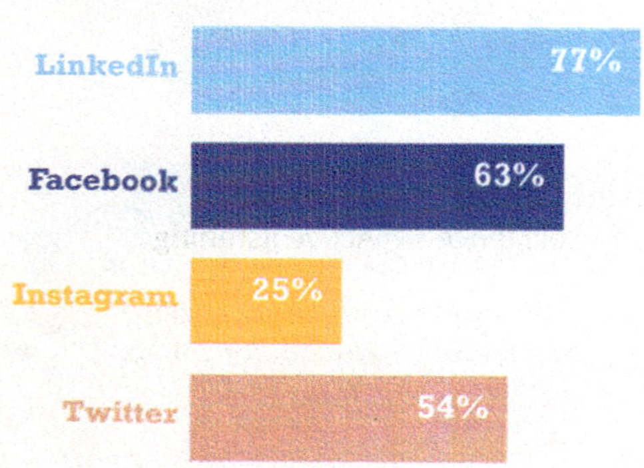

35% of millennial recruiters and 63% of tech industry recruiters use Instagram to find suitable candidates.

21% of recruiters say that candidates with a social media presence have a greater chance of getting an interview than those without.

- Are any of these statistics surprising to you? Which ones? Why?
- Have you used any social media sites in your job search? Which ones? What happened?
- Do you think any particular site is better for job searching? Which one? Why?

Step 7 Going forward

A PAIRS **In your online course, you reflected on how you could improve your online professional profile after studying more about job search by using LinkedIn. Discuss. Listen to the example.**

B SHARE **Present your ideas to the class.**

VOCABULARY PRACTICE
Go to page 84.

I can explain how to use social media for job search. ☐

12 MODULE

Interviewing

Evaluating Job Offers

DISCUSSION STRATEGIES
Go to page 68.

Step 1 Get started

A Refresh your memory! Watch the *What You'll Learn* video.

B Look at the photo. What are the main factors that job seekers should consider before accepting a job offer?

C Check your understanding. Go to page 65.

Step 2 Tell your story

A THINK In your online course, you thought about a time when you (or someone you know) considered a job offer. What affected your decision to accept or reject it? Listen to the example.

B PAIRS Discuss your story.

C SHARE Tell your story to the class.

Step 3 Take away

A PAIRS Review your notes from the online module and complete the checklist about how to evaluate job offers with the words in the box.

costs	discounts	employees	established	policies
reimbursement	standard	subsidized	tasks	

- ☑ the [1] ____________ benefits – e.g., vacation time, sick pay, holidays, etc.
- ☑ any additional benefits – e.g., [2] ____________ meals or transportation costs, employee [3] ____________, bonuses, annual pay raises, tuition [4] ____________ plans
- ☑ the job location – consider transportation [5] ____________ and commuting time
- ☑ the company – is it [6] ____________, new, or growing?
- ☑ the culture – its values, beliefs, [7] ____________, and social programs
- ☑ the people – the other [8] ____________ you'd be working with
- ☑ the job description – what your daily [9] ____________ would be

B SHARE Check your answers with the class. Would you add more considerations to the checklist?

Step 4 Activate your knowledge

A PAIRS Read the three scenarios about people deciding which job to choose. Then complete the chart of pros and cons for each scenario.

SCENARIO 1 After graduating with a bachelor's degree in educational technology, **Esin** moved to a bigger city, applied for jobs, and received two offers. She has to choose one right away in order to continue to pay her rent and basic expenses. The first offer is as a specialist at a distance education department of a university. It's an entry-level position with a low annual salary, which would cover her rent with only a little left over. The main benefits would include subsidized meals, a minimum annual pay raise of 20%, and a 75% tuition discount if she pursues a Master's degree in the educational technology program. The second offer is from an education company that provides digital products to schools. The salary would be higher, and they'd pay for her transportation costs. She'd be eligible for quarterly bonuses, too. Esin isn't sure which option is the best choice?

SCENARIO 1	PROS	CONS
Job offer 1		
Job offer 2		

SCENARIO 2 **Hue** has been working as a front desk receptionist at a five-star hotel for over five years now. She enjoys meeting and working with different people at her job. The culture of the hotel is warm and friendly, and she gets 15 vacation days a year. The only problem is that she doesn't see herself as a receptionist for the long-term, so she's planning a career change. Given her experience in a fast-paced, client-facing environment, she believes she could be successful in sales. So, she had a couple of interviews and received an offer as an entry-level sales associate for a bedding company, whose products are used at the hotel she works at. The annual salary is less than her current job, and she would only get five vacation days each year. She'd have to work by herself a lot as she visited different clients. On the other hand, the company invests in its staff's professional development by providing regular in-house trainings and tuition reimbursement for business- and sales-related courses taken elsewhere. She doesn't know whether or not to accept the offer.

SCENARIO 2	PROS	CONS
Current job		
Job offer		

SCENARIO 3 **Miguel** has worked as a senior accountant at an established, successful clothing company for about ten years. He enjoys the job and likes the company. The office is also close to home. However, he's been working in the same position for four years now, and it seems he won't get a promotion in the near future unless someone leaves or retires. He was recently contacted by a recruiter and offered an executive-level position in the finance department of a newly founded company that's a competitor in the same industry. They've offered him a salary almost 40% higher than what he is currently earning. They also offered him a company car since he'd have to visit another office once a week, and it takes almost two hours to get there. The company offers employee discounts on its products, like his current employer, but it also has an annual bonus plan, which his current company does not. Miguel is enticed by the offer, but he is uncertain.

SCENARIO 3	PROS	CONS
Current job		
Job offer		

B PAIRS **Discuss which job you think each person should choose and why.**

C GROUPS **Join another group to compare your answers for each scenario.**

Step 5 Project

A PAIRS In your online course, you ranked a list of criteria for evaluating a job offer and explained why you would prioritize them that way. Share your lists and reasons. Read the example.

Right now, my husband and I are planning to have a baby, so my top priorities when evaluating job offers would be a flexible work schedule, health insurance, family leave, and childcare services. I would also like a job that isn't far from my home.

B SHARE Compare your lists and priorities as a class.

Step 6 Talk!

PAIRS Job seekers consider a number of factors before accepting a job offer. Read the main factors job seekers consider. Then discuss the questions.

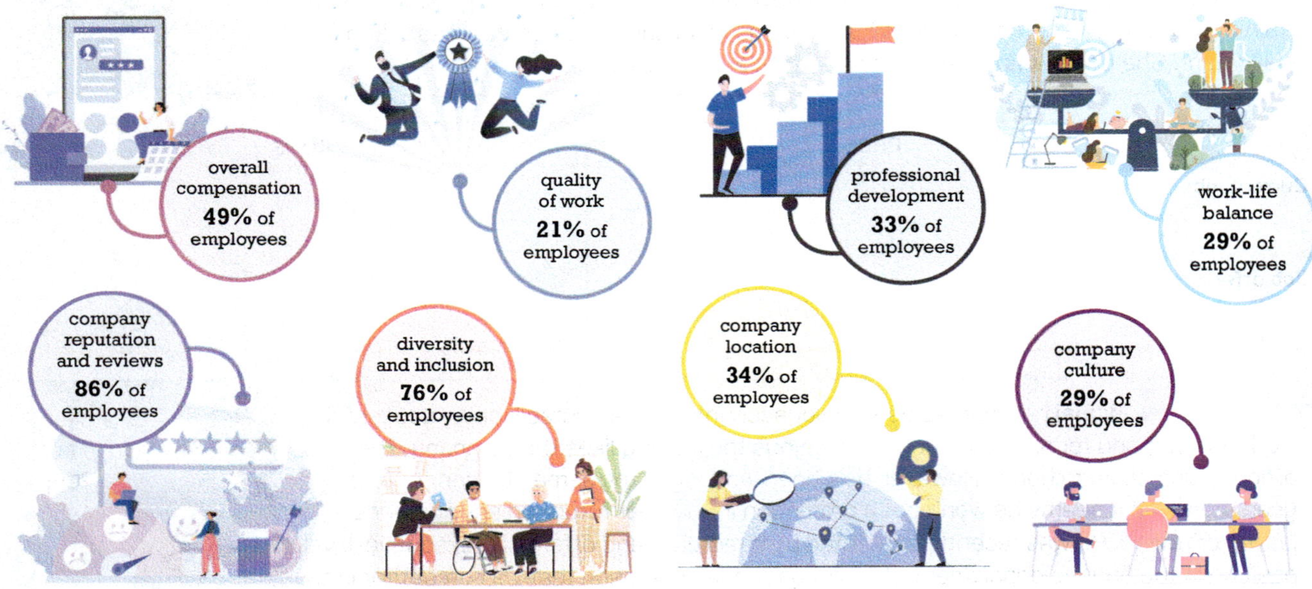

- Do you find any of these facts surprising? Which ones? Why?
- Which of these factors are most important to you? Why?
- Are there other factors that are important to you that are not on the list? What are they?

Step 7 Going forward

A PAIRS In your online course, you reflected on evaluating job offers after studying more about it. Discuss. Listen to the example.

B SHARE Present your ideas to the class.

VOCABULARY PRACTICE
Go to page 85.

I can describe the criteria for evaluating a job offer. ☐

CHECK YOUR UNDERSTANDING

Check your understanding 1

REFRESH YOUR MEMORY!

Review the Online Course material in your Resources.

Choose the best answers. More than one answer may be correct in some items.

1 **Nonverbal communication is ____.**

a conveying messages through body language
b communicating through email
c thinking about something you want to say

2 **It is important to use and interpret body language correctly at work so that you ____.**

a don't misunderstand someone's meaning
b can communicate meaning accurately
c can be considered for promotions

3 **Some examples of posture are ____.**

a smiling, frowning, or rolling your eyes
b giving a thumbs-up or a thumbs-down
c standing up straight or leaning forward

4 **What can be understood if someone avoids making eye contact?**

a They are uninterested in what you are saying.
b They are surprised at what you are saying.
c They don't understand what you are saying.

5 **____ can show that you are worried or nervous.**

a Fidgeting
b Biting your lip
c Crossing your arms

6 **Usually, an appropriate physical distance means standing ____ the other person.**

a shoulder to shoulder with
b an arm's length away from
c a body's length away from

7 **Sarah is attending a conference for franchise managers from around the world. When meeting with international franchise owners, what would be helpful for Sarah to remember about non-verbal communication?**

a Different cultures may have different interpretations of facial expressions and/or gestures, so be aware of these possible differences to avoid misunderstanding.
b Smiling is important to make people believe you are happy with them and what they are saying, so smile even when you disagree.
c Pay attention to how close you stand when talking to other people to make sure that they are not feeling uncomfortable.

8 **Peter is an electrical technician. He is trying to explain an electrical problem to a customer. The customer is making eye contact and wrinkling his forehead. This might mean the customer ____.**

a is not interested in what Peter is saying
b needs Peter to explain the problem in simpler terms
c is frustrated and annoyed because of the problem

9 **Henry is a receptionist at a nursing home. He has a meeting with the office manager one day, but he is feeling tired because he did not sleep well the night before. During the meeting, he slouches down in his chair because he is too tired to sit straight. The office manager might interpret this behavior as Henry ____.**

a feeling nervous or shy
b feeling bored or not caring
c hiding his real feelings

10 **Tania is a plumber. One of her clients gets upset one day and tells her she seems uninterested in helping him. What might she have done to give this negative impression?
While the client was describing the problem, she ____.**

a looked away and studied the room
b wrinkled her forehead and bit her lip
c crossed her arms and smiled

Check your understanding 2

REFRESH YOUR MEMORY!

Review the Online Course material in your Resources.

Choose the best answers. More than one answer may be correct in some items.

1 In which situations is it important to be able to communicate persuasively at work?

a when preparing a marketing campaign
b when presenting ideas in a meeting
c when researching competitors' products

2 Which of Aristotle's three tools of persuasion refers to using emotion to appeal to your audience?

a logos
b ethos
c pathos

3 Which of Cialdini's principles of persuasion refers to the idea that people tend to be more willing to give something if they have received something?

a reciprocity
b authority
c liking someone

4 Funneling is ____.

a the technique of asking effective questions to determine the best solution for a customer
b a way of using logic to make people do things they normally wouldn't want to do
c a way of finding out people's inner motivations and using them to make a persuasive argument

5 Why is storytelling a persuasive technique?

a It engages your audience.
b It is used by many persuasive speakers.
c It makes the speaker likeable.

6 To develop your powers of persuasion, it can help to ____.

a memorize some good anecdotes to share whenever you are speaking
b pay attention to the techniques that effective speakers use
c create a list of the various techniques so you can remember them

7 Tony is a sales person in a large department store. A customer comes in looking for a new coffee machine. She isn't sure what features she wants. What would be the best technique for Tony to use to figure out which machine he can sell to her?

a storytelling
b funneling
c pathos

8 Daisy works at the front desk of a large hotel. During a meeting with the other hotel workers, she wants to pitch an idea for a new, more personalized check-in method for guests. She engages the other workers and their manager by telling a personalized anecdote and using emotional words. What persuasive strategies is she using?

a storytelling
b funneling
c pathos

9 Jaden manages a team of researchers in a biology lab. He is proposing a new project to the team. As he presents the research topic, he invites comments and listens attentively to questions from the team. This creates an atmosphere of trust and respect. What persuasive technique does Jaden's behavior illustrate?

a the principle of reciprocity
b the principle of authority
c asking effective questions

10 Lena owns a hair salon. Around holidays, she often offers chocolates and other small treats to her clients. Her clients love these small surprises, and they often tell their friends about the salon. What persuasive technique does this illustrate?

a the principle of reciprocity
b the principle of authority
c ethos

Check your understanding 3

REFRESH YOUR MEMORY!

Review the Online Course material in your Resources.

Choose the best answers. More than one answer may be correct in some items.

1 What question should you ask yourself when setting a goal?
- **a** Why is this goal important to me?
- **b** How does this goal relate to my personal ambitions?
- **c** Who will reward me for working toward this goal?

2 Why is it important to set and commit to goals?
- **a** It helps you complete many tasks at once.
- **b** It helps you stay focused on what is important.
- **c** It makes you feel confident and resilient.

3 What are some common actions that make it difficult to stay committed to goals?
- **a** creating an overwhelming situation by setting too many goals
- **b** not setting enough goals to get excited about them
- **c** putting off tasks because they feel scary or overwhelming

4 If you are too busy to make time for goals, you should ____.
- **a** put the goal off until a later date when you might have time
- **b** try to drop one activity to make time for your goal
- **c** schedule regular time into your calendar to work toward the goal

5 It helps to talk about your goal with someone else because that person can ____.
- **a** help you remember to work toward your goal
- **b** motivate you by working together with you
- **c** help you determine what the goal should be

6 When you achieve a step toward your goal, what should you do?
- **a** Move quickly on to the next step on your list.
- **b** Pause to complete any tools and training you need.
- **c** Reward yourself for the accomplishment as a way to stay motivated.

7 Celine has several goals that she wants to achieve. She wants to get her business degree, learn a second language, and get a full-time job. To achieve her goals, Celine needs to ____.
- **a** list the goals in order of priority and not try to focus on all of them at once
- **b** list the steps needed for each goal and work on them simultaneously
- **c** make sure the goals align with the vision she has for her life

8 Peter works as a sales assistant. He works full-time on weekdays, and on weekends he spends time with friends. Peter wants to get a degree in education and become a teacher. He has the application forms for a few graduate programs, but he hasn't filled them in yet. Which strategies might help Peter commit to his goal?
- **a** He can get tools and training before he fills in the applications.
- **b** He can try blocking off time on his calendar to fill out the applications.
- **c** He should talk to a friend or family member who could help support and encourage him.

9 Beth wants to become a translator. She knows three different languages and she is studying a fourth. She has put together a portfolio of articles that she has translated, and she has identified some companies where she might like to work. She has set a schedule to work on her résumé and job applications. Which statement is true about Beth's situation?
- **a** She will likely be successful because she has set practical, achievable goals.
- **b** She might get overwhelmed because she has set too many goals for herself.
- **c** She needs to stop procrastinating if she wants to achieve her goal.

10 Juan has just graduated from university with a degree in graphic design. He is having trouble deciding what kind of job he should apply for. His father is insisting that he be a website designer for a large corporation, but Juan thinks he might be happier working for a smaller design firm. Which statement is true about Juan's situation?
- **a** His father's support will help Juan achieve his goal.
- **b** Juan needs to figure out what goal aligns with his vision for himself.
- **c** If Juan puts off working toward a goal, he can figure out what he wants.

Check your understanding 4

REFRESH YOUR MEMORY!

Review the Online Course material in your Resources.

Choose the best answers. More than one answer may be correct in some items.

1 Emotional intelligence refers to ____.

a awareness and understanding of your feelings

b feeling strongly about things

c being able to perceive the feelings of others

2 Which component of emotional intelligence refers to the ability to do tasks without needing persuasion or praise from others?

a self-regulation

b intrinsic motivation

c social skills

3 If someone is able to understand other people's feelings, this is called ____.

a intrinsic motivation

b empathy

c social skills

4 Why is it important for a team to have high emotional intelligence?

a They are more engaged and can work more effectively together.

b Their understanding of others' emotions can help prevent conflict.

c They can come up with innovative ideas quickly.

5 Members of a team with high emotional intelligence ____.

a make each other feel safe and welcome

b don't often get upset about making mistakes

c learn from mistakes and avoid blaming each other

6 To build emotional intelligence, team members can ____.

a explain the rules clearly to new members

b give each other constructive feedback

c make sure that each member has a way to contribute to the team

7 Carol, Joe, and Dani work in a hospital and are preparing a training for staff. They agree to each bring a suggested training agenda to their first meeting. When they meet, their agendas are very different. They first share the reasoning behind their agendas and from that start to agree the course content. How is their team showing emotional intelligence?

a They are engaging in the project, showing intrinsic motivation.

b They are listening openly to each other's ideas, showing empathy and social skills.

c They are learning from their mistakes and moving forward, showing self-regulation.

8 Darla, Tom, and Otto are the principals of an elementary, middle, and high school within one district. They are working together to draft a mission statement and long-term goals for the district. Darla is having a hard time focusing on the team goals due to a series of worrying personal issues. How can the team manage this problem in an emotionally intelligent way?

a Darla can try to self-regulate by acknowledging her own feelings and trying to control them.

b Tom can acknowledge Darla's feelings and set up a time to discuss the issue.

c Otto can ask Darla to come to meetings only when she can put her feelings aside.

9 Meltem, Greta, and Oscar work at a non-profit group that provides assistance after natural disasters. They are creating a budget for the upcoming year. Greta's accounting skills are not strong, and she is nervous about working with numbers, but she wants to contribute. The team can manage this issue in an emotionally intelligent way by ____.

a having Greta work on the big-picture aspects of the budget, which she feels more comfortable with

b asking Greta just to watch the process, without working on it, so that she can learn from it

c trying to ignore any mistakes Greta makes in the budget process

10 David, Hugo, and Maria are on a business course, and are working together on their final project. They all have full courseloads, so have decided to hold weekly progress meetings. Hugo often misses the meetings, and David and Maria are frustrated by this and feel that he isn't contributing. The team can manage this problem in an emotionally intelligent way by ____.

a telling Hugo that he is creating a problem for the team

b talking to Hugo and finding out why he is not always able to attend

c asking Hugo how he would like to and be able to contribute to the project

Check your understanding 5

REFRESH YOUR MEMORY!

Review the Online Course material in your Resources.

Choose the best answers. More than one answer may be correct in some items.

1 **Key differences between low-risk and high-risk decisions are that high-risk decisions ____.**

a can be made by intuition alone

b can have serious consequences

c involve critical thinking skills

2 **After identifying a decision, the next three steps in making a good decision are ____.**

a gather data, consider the options, and evaluate possible outcomes

b choose the best option, evaluate possible outcomes, and act on the decision

c gather data, act on the decision, and review the decision

3 **Which two statements about decision-making are myths?**

a It's always a bad idea to make a quick decision.

b It's important to list every possible option before making a decision.

c It's good to consider carefully who needs to be included in the decision making.

4 **Cecilia owns a line of hair salons. She wants these to become more environmentally friendly, so she is considering changing the products they use. She is currently researching different brands, finding information on ingredients used, production methods, and on people's satisfaction with the quality of the product. Which step of the decision-making process is this?**

a Identify the decision

b Gather data

c Consider the options

5 **Peter is the head librarian of his town's library, and is trying to decide the best use for a new space. He could use it for more books, which the library always needs. But using it for computers might be more useful. A third option, using the space for public events, might attract more people to the library. Which step of the decision-making process is this?**

a Identify the decision

b Gather data

c Evaluate possible outcomes

6 **The managers of an elder care facility are evaluating which cleaning company to hire. They have a list of twenty local agencies and plan to do a comparison study of the three with the best online reviews. One of the managers, Gianna, thinks they need to be more thorough, and look at all twenty of the companies. Which myth of decision-making is Gianna believing?**

a Decisions made quickly are bad decisions.

b Every possible option should be analyzed.

c Everyone should be involved in the decision-making process.

7 **The IT department of a university wants to update their classroom technology. They have considered different technological solutions, and they have made a decision based on the cost, number of classrooms, and overall reliability of the different options. They are putting the order through now. Which step of the decision-making process is this?**

a Choose the best option

b Act on the decision

c Review the decision

8 **The administrative team at a private high school has decided, based on parent feedback, that they need to change their catering company. They are looking at several different options and making notes about factors such as variety of food, quality of food, and price. They still have more options they want to research. Which step of the decision-making process is this?**

a Gather data

b Consider the options

c Evaluate possible outcomes

9 **John owns a small clothing store. Over the past few years, he has been losing business to some of the larger department stores as well as to online retailers. He wants to come up with some innovative ideas that will draw people in to his store. Now he needs to figure out what some possible new ideas for his store are. Which step of the decision-making process is this?**

a Identify the decision

b Gather data

c Consider the options

Check your understanding 6

REFRESH YOUR MEMORY!

Review the Online Course material in your Resources.

Choose the best answers. More than one answer may be correct in some items.

1 **It is important to understand the pros and cons of different leadership styles in order to _____.**

a understand which style is most suitable for a particular situation

b make sure that people will follow your orders without questioning them

c feel safe expressing your opinion in certain situations

2 **Which leadership style is most useful in emergencies or military operations?**

a autocratic

b participative

c transactional

3 **Which leadership style might slow down processes and decisions?**

a autocratic

b participative

c transactional

4 **With the _____ leadership style, the leader uses a hands-off approach, letting others manage tasks.**

a autocratic

b participative

c delegative

5 **When a company is going through major changes, one of the most effective types of leader is a _____ leader.**

a delegative

b transactional

c transformational

6 **Sales teams often follow a _____ type of leadership, in which short-term goals are prioritized and rewards may be given for meeting targets.**

a participative

b transactional

c transformational

7 **Nam-gil works in the marketing department of an internet service provider, and was recently promoted. He is a hard worker and tends to do all tasks himself. But he understands that in a management role, the amount of work he has will be too much to do alone, and he needs to give his team members the ability to grow. To develop his leadership style, he can _____.**

a ask his supervisor to mentor him as he becomes accustomed to his new leadership role

b ask his friends and colleagues to tell him what leadership style he should use

c reflect on the different leadership styles and consider which situations they will work best in

8 **Han works for a construction company. When he is managing a site, he often walks around to check workers are following the safety protocols and tells them what to do when he sees a problem. Han feels this is the most efficient way to get the job done, but the workers think he doesn't trust them. This has created low morale. Han's dominant leadership style is _____.**

a autocratic

b delegative

c transactional

9 **Sarah is responsible for fundraising at a local environmental group. To help the group reach its annual goal, Sarah gives each volunteer a personal target. To motivate the volunteers, Sarah gives incentives for those who meet their targets, and gives small prizes to the volunteers who bring in the most new donors. Sarah's dominant leadership style is _____.**

a participative

b transactional

c transformational

10 **Viktor is a lead architect at a mid-sized firm. When he has a project, he gives tasks to each of the junior architects in the team he manages. Viktor meets with each of them regularly to go over questions and give them guidance. They are excited at the chance to grow on the job and improve their skills under his mentorship. Viktor's dominant leadership style is _____.**

a delegative

b participative

c transactional

Check your understanding 7

REFRESH YOUR MEMORY!

Review the Online Course material in your Resources.

Choose the best answers. More than one answer may be correct in some items.

1 Some characteristics of soft deadlines are ____.

- **a** they are flexible
- **b** they can help us work toward hard deadlines
- **c** they are usually set by other people

2 What are some benefits of deadlines?

- **a** Having a deadline can make people stop procrastinating.
- **b** Having a deadline can make people feel less anxious about work.
- **c** Meeting deadlines can help people build a good reputation.

3 What are useful strategies for meeting hard deadlines on a large project?

- **a** Give yourself time to think about the project before starting.
- **b** Break the large project down into smaller pieces.
- **c** Set interim deadlines and assign a reasonable amount of time for each.

4 When setting deadlines, it is important to ____.

- **a** try to create a schedule that aims for the best-case scenario
- **b** be careful not to underestimate the amount of time needed for tasks
- **c** allow extra time in case of unexpected delays

5 What are some strategies to help you meet deadlines?

- **a** Begin work as soon as possible.
- **b** Don't worry about interim soft deadlines.
- **c** Track the time it takes you to complete tasks.

6 When you are having trouble meeting a deadline, ____.

- **a** ask for extra time as soon as possible
- **b** eliminate non-essential tasks
- **c** revise the schedule as often as you can

7 Min manages a creative team at an advertising agency. The agency has a new client and Min's team has to prepare a presentation. They have two weeks to put something together, and Min knows that a lot of time is needed for the creative process. To make sure the team is ready on time, Min can ____.

- **a** give each team member a tight schedule to be sure they finish
- **b** assign interim deadlines to keep the team moving forward
- **c** review the schedule often and if necessary, ask the client for an extension

8 Alex has a full-time job and is also taking a college business course online. He has a big end-of-term project to finish, which he has known about for a month. He broke it down into smaller parts, assigning himself interim deadlines, but he was busy and never found the time for it. The project is due tomorrow, and he knows he can't finish in time. Alex could have ____.

- **a** asked his professor sooner whether an extension would be possible
- **b** broken down the work into more manageable pieces
- **c** scheduled a small amount of time each day and set reminders for himself

9 Jen leads a legal research team for a law firm. Their current case has a court date four weeks from now. Jen has broken the research into pieces, assigned each assistant a piece, and set a soft deadline of two weeks for each to do their piece. She has set up weekly status meetings with the team until the court date. Jen will likely meet her deadline because she ____.

- **a** has made time to ask for an extension if necessary
- **b** has built in extra time which will help in case of delays
- **c** is reviewing the team's work regularly so she can track progress

10 Mila wanted to start her own fashion design business. She was having trouble making the time to focus on creating the new designs she needed. Then she found out about a fashion show for local artists, applied, and was accepted to show her work. Now she has a hard deadline to get her designs done. Having a deadline might help Mila by giving her ____.

- **a** the motivation she needs to get her designs done
- **b** a way to have a positive attitude toward deadlines
- **c** more confidence once she meets the deadline

Check your understanding 8

REFRESH YOUR MEMORY!
Review the Online Course material in your Resources.

Choose the best answers. More than one answer may be correct in some items.

1 **Having a good work-life balance means ____.**
- **a** keeping your work life and your personal life separate
- **b** working no more than forty hours per week
- **c** prioritizing family and friends over work responsibilities

2 **A good work-life balance may ____.**
- **a** make people a little less productive at work
- **b** help keep people from getting stressed out
- **c** give people time to exercise

3 **What are some ways of achieving work-life balance?**
- **a** learning how to multi-task more frequently
- **b** making time for relaxing and fun activities
- **c** rewarding yourself for achievements

4 **In order to correct an imbalance in your work-life balance, it is important to ____.**
- **a** pinpoint what is causing the stress
- **b** be willing to talk honestly about it
- **c** work only in an office

5 **Valerio is a video editor. He works long hours from his home office, not taking breaks for lunch and ending late in the evening. He often takes on more projects than he can really manage. On the weekends, he is too exhausted to enjoy his free time, and spends most of his time on social media. Valerio can restore his work-life balance by ____.**
- **a** trying to make a separate area for his work so he doesn't get distracted
- **b** setting priorities so that he doesn't have too many projects at once
- **c** rewarding himself with short breaks after completing each task

6 **Tara is an auto mechanic who works independently out of her garage. She is always very busy and often works late, missing dinner with her family. She also works on weekends to take care of repairs she couldn't finish during the week. She has recently started feeling depressed and can't sleep at night. Tara can restore her work-life balance by ____.**
- **a** trying to identify why she is stressed and having sleepless nights
- **b** taking a break at dinnertime to spend time with her family
- **c** concentrating on her tasks and watching TV while she works

7 **Sasha is an industrial designer for a toy company. During her workday, she is always busy with meetings, and with reviewing the work of the junior designers she manages. She has very little time to think creatively. She has decided to start waking up half an hour earlier every day to go for a jog. This might help her restore her work-life balance because she'll ____.**
- **a** have more energy
- **b** feel rewarded for her work
- **c** feel restored

8 **To support his family, Salvo is a customer service representative at a call center during the days, and a security guard in the evenings. He comes home late and tired. On the weekends, he spends time with his family and helps around the house. Salvo enjoys this, but is exhausted and starting to feel depressed. Salvo can correct his work-life imbalance by ____.**
- **a** trying to identify the source of his stress
- **b** focusing only on essential tasks at work
- **c** talking to his family about his stress

Check your understanding 9

REFRESH YOUR MEMORY!

Review the Online Course material in your Resources.

Choose the best answers. More than one answer may be correct in some items.

1 **In an ethically strong workplace, ____.**

- **a** decisions are made based on a set of principles and values
- **b** workers try to maintain a fair, open, and responsible workplace
- **c** workers are told what decisions they should make in various situations

2 **A document that describes a company's core values, such as inclusivity or being respectful, is known as a ____.**

- **a** PLUS model
- **b** code of ethics
- **c** code of conduct

3 **A document that lists specific behaviors that are acceptable or unacceptable, such as not accepting bribes, is called a ____.**

- **a** PLUS model
- **b** code of ethics
- **c** code of conduct

4 **Making an ethical decision is not always straightforward because ____.**

- **a** several different factors need to be considered
- **b** people might disagree on what is right or wrong
- **c** too many employees act unethically

5 **What four factors are considered when using the PLUS method of ethical decision making?**

- **a** the company's policies, the law, what people usually do, and what you yourself think
- **b** the company's policies, the law, the company's universal values, and your own values
- **c** possible benefits for the company, the law, the company's values, and the simplest solution

6 **Peter works in a college admissions office. Recently, he learned that an accepted student lied about her volunteer experience on her application. The student had good grades, but the college's policy is not to accept students who are not truthful. He writes to the student and tells her that she is no longer accepted. Which step of the PLUS method has Peter considered?**

a P **b** L **c** U **d** S

7 **Carl is a salesclerk at an electronics store. He has a co-worker who makes jokes about other workers' ages. This bothers Carl, who thinks respecting people is important. The store has no specific policy about jokes, but it does have a mission of promoting a respectful workplace. Carl decides to talk to his co-worker. Which steps of the PLUS method has Carl considered?**

a P **b** L **c** U **d** S

8 **Luisa manages a café where there is an understanding that at the end of the day, the workers share out the tips equally. Luisa has noticed that one of the workers, Dale, often takes extra. The café has no formal code of conduct, but Luisa wants everyone to treat each other fairly. She decides to talk to Dale. Which step of the PLUS model does Dale's behavior violate?**

a P **b** L **c** U **d** S

9 **One day at the office, Jo notices a colleague has left a job application for a different company on the printer. Company policy is not to use company resources for personal use. But Jo doesn't want to violate the employee's privacy. She decides to bring the application to her colleague discreetly and not report it. Which steps of the PLUS method has Jo considered?**

a P **b** L **c** U **d** S

Check your understanding 10

REFRESH YOUR MEMORY!
Review the Online Course material in your Resources.

Choose the best answers. More than one answer may be correct in some items.

1 An elevator pitch is a ____.
- a brief presentation about yourself
- b conversation you have with someone in an elevator
- c list of all your personal accomplishments

2 You should have an elevator pitch so that you ____.
- a remember things about the job you are you trying to get
- b have more confidence in approaching people you want to impress
- c focus on what matters and come across as authentic

3 Which places are appropriate for using an elevator pitch?
- a a recruitment fair
- b a conference
- c a business meeting

4 How could you start your elevator pitch effectively?
- a "Hi, I'd like to introduce myself."
- b "I've been waiting to speak with you."
- c "Excuse me. Do you have a minute?"

5 What should you make sure to include in an elevator pitch?
- a your name and what you do
- b a list of all the awards you have received
- c what you are hoping to achieve

6 After coming up with your elevator pitch, you should ____.
- a memorize it and not change it again or you might forget it
- b rehearse it often and ask friends or family for feedback
- c modify it to fit particular audiences as well as changes in your career

7 Junjie works in marketing for a telecommunications company. At a networking event he approaches the CEO from a global company that he would like to work for. She seems busy, so he says, "Excuse me" and then immediately starts talking about his accomplishments. The CEO seems confused and walks away quickly. What did Junjie do wrong?
- a He didn't wait for a good moment.
- b He forgot to introduce himself.
- c He approached the CEO at the wrong kind of event.

8 Akiko has just completed a course in fashion design. She is attending a networking event at a fashion show. While standing in line to get coffee, she sees a famous designer in front of her. She is nervous but wants to talk to him, and she has practiced a pitch for this kind of opportunity. What factors might help Akiko succeed?
- a She is at the right type of event to approach the designer.
- b Having rehearsed her pitch will help her sound confident.
- c Her experience helps her stand apart from others.

9 Luz is a web designer. She works independently but would like to join a design firm. She goes to a job fair and speaks with various companies, each of which has a different specialty. Luz has memorized and rehearsed her elevator pitch, which is about 40 seconds long, and she delivers it the same way to each person she speaks with. To improve, Luz needs to ____.
- a focus just on one or two companies and say more to each
- b target her pitch specifically to different companies
- c lengthen her pitch so that she can be more persuasive

10 Ken is a landscaper. He needs a job, so he decides to go to a recruitment fair. He wants to be prepared so that he will come across as professional and get some good opportunities. To prepare a good elevator pitch, he can ____.
- a write down a 500-word pitch and memorize it
- b record himself and analyze his performance
- c make sure his body language makes him look authentic

Check your understanding 11

REFRESH YOUR MEMORY!

Review the Online Course material in your Resources.

Choose the best answers. More than one answer may be correct in some items.

1 **LinkedIn is ____.**

- **a** one of the largest online professional networking sites
- **b** a résumé building website for job seekers
- **c** a social media site used by businesses and individuals

2 **Why do people use LinkedIn?**

- **a** to build a professional network
- **b** to look for job opportunities
- **c** to meet up with friends for social events

3 **How can you use LinkedIn for your job search?**

- **a** Filter your search by looking for people you know on LinkedIn.
- **b** Use key words such as a job title in the search bar to search job postings.
- **c** Find a job you want and apply directly through LinkedIn.

4 **Your LinkedIn profile is different from your résumé because it ____.**

- **a** is not tailored to a specific job
- **b** highlights particular skills
- **c** shows your work experience

5 **What should your LinkedIn profile include?**

- **a** a professional photo and a summary of your accomplishments
- **b** a cover letter that states your objectives and highlights your experience
- **c** a list of relevant skills and at least two recommendations

6 **In order to keep your LinkedIn profile relevant, ____.**

- **a** keep your list of skills limited to three or four
- **b** review and revise your skills regularly
- **c** include recommendations from colleagues and family members

7 **Maruwan is a mechanical engineer. He is creating a LinkedIn profile for himself and needs to add a photo. He should use ____.**

- **a** an old high school photo, in which he looks serious but friendly
- **b** a photo from vacation last summer, in which he is turning to look at a friend and laughing
- **c** a photo he took with his webcam, in which he is smiling and looking at the camera

8 **Cecilia is a photographer. She is creating a LinkedIn profile and has written a short summary outlining the type of work she normally does, and a few of her strongest personal qualities related to her photography work, such as how she can make clients feel at ease. Cecilia's summary is still a little short, and she wants to extend it. She should add ____.**

- **a** a list of some photography awards she has received
- **b** a list of all the clients she has worked for in the past
- **c** her professional objectives and goals

9 **Tal is studying to be a psychotherapist. He has had several part-time jobs in the past, and so he has acquired a wide variety of skills. When he finishes his studies, he would like to set up his own practice as a therapist. When setting up his LinkedIn profile, he should include ____.**

- **a** all of his skills, regardless of the field
- **b** only general skills which could be applied to several different fields
- **c** skills which are specifically relevant to the field of psychotherapy

10 **Maya is a massage therapist at a spa. She updates her LinkedIn profile regularly and is always looking out for job opportunities. Recently, the spa hired another therapist. Maya finds this person very professional and kind, and they work well together. Maya added the person to her LinkedIn profile. To help her friend and strengthen her own profile, she could ____.**

- **a** write a recommendation and ask for one in return
- **b** copy some of the ideas from her friend's profile on her own
- **c** endorse her friend's skills and ask for an endorsement of her own

Check your understanding 12

REFRESH YOUR MEMORY!
Review the Online Course material in your Resources.

Choose the best answers. More than one answer may be correct in some items.

1 **It is important to evaluate job offers because it helps ____.**
- **a** determine the choice between two offers
- **b** first-time job seekers find the right job
- **c** determine the salary you need to cover expenses

2 **When evaluating a job's pay and benefits, what should you consider?**
- **a** The salary is the most important factor; the job with the highest pay is usually the best choice.
- **b** It's important to think about your particular situation and which benefits might help you most.
- **c** Look carefully at the job offer to see if there are benefits beyond the basic ones.

3 **Some standard benefits that most companies offer are ____.**
- **a** paid holidays
- **b** accident pay
- **c** tuition reimbursement

4 **When evaluating the company itself, you should consider ____.**
- **a** what the long-term prospects are
- **b** what the company culture is like
- **c** how many employees they are currently hiring

5 **You can learn about a company's culture by ____.**
- **a** asking about it at your interview
- **b** checking where the company is located
- **c** looking at the company's website

6 **When evaluating a job, you should also consider ____.**
- **a** your daily tasks and who you will work with
- **b** what your instinct is telling you about the job
- **c** where you found the information about the job

7 **Liz, a mother of two, teaches part-time at a local school. The pay is not great, but she likes her colleagues. Recently, she was offered a full-time job with better pay at another school. If she accepts the offer, her family would have to move to another city. She would also have to teach classes she has not taught before. Liz might reject the offer because of ____.**
- **a** the pay and benefits
- **b** the people and job
- **c** the location and her personal situation

8 **When Tomas graduated in economics, he received two job offers. One was with a large bank with good pay and opportunities for advancement. The other was with a smaller, growing bank. The pay was not as good, but they offered professional development. Tomas liked the interviewer, and the employees looked happy. He accepted the job at the smaller bank because ____.**
- **a** he had a gut feeling about what the company culture would be
- **b** the salary and the benefits were the most important consideration for him
- **c** he was looking for a company where he could be promoted quickly

9 **Min-ji has a degree in childhood education. She has just received a part-time, hourly job offer from a childcare facility. She would not get paid sick days or holidays, but after three years, she could become a full-time worker. The other employees seemed stressed out. So, Min-ji has decided to wait for another offer. In evaluating this job, she considered the ____.**
- **a** benefits
- **b** culture
- **c** location

10 **Rober is an architect at a small firm. He loves his job, but the pay is not great, and he works long hours. He is thinking of starting a family, so he has applied to some other firms and received an offer. The new job would pay better, and he could work regular hours. But the work would not be very interesting. When evaluating the new job, Rober should consider ____.**
- **a** how far it is from his family
- **b** his personal situation
- **c** the salary

DISCUSSION STRATEGIES

Discussion strategies

When you are in class or at work, you may need to take part in discussions. To successfully participate, you can use a number of different kinds of strategies. They include strategies that help you:

1 Work with others
2 Clarify what you hear or clarify what you say
3 Get and stay involved in the discussion
4 Organize your ideas

During each discussion in class, choose one kind of strategy you want to improve or one you think will be useful. Pick a phrase and try to use it during the in-class activities. Remember to always say the phrase in a polite way.

You can listen to the phrases and examples ▶.

1 Working with others

Some strategies can make it easier to work with other people who are part of the discussion. If you can, try starting the discussion or helping to keep the discussion moving in the right direction. These strategies can help.

Management strategies	Sample phrases
a Starting the discussion	▶ Is everyone ready? ▶ Let's get going. ▶ Who wants to get us started?
b Asking others to participate	▶ Who wants to share any thoughts? ▶ Does anyone have anything to add? ▶ Who wants to contribute next?
c Helping specific people to get involved	▶ Marco, what do you think? ▶ Do you have anything to add, Chen? ▶ Karina, any opinions on this?
d Jumping in with talkative people	▶ That's a good point, but it would be great to hear from everyone else. ▶ OK, thanks! And what about everyone else? ▶ Great point, Alana! Now, why don't we see what some others think?
e Staying on the topic	▶ That's interesting, but maybe I'm missing something. I don't see how that contributes to our topic. ▶ Let's discuss this later. For now, we need to stay on task if we're going to finish on time. ▶ Sorry, but I don't think that's really going to help us with this topic.
f Keeping the discussion moving	▶ OK. So now let's move on to the next issue [on our agenda]. ▶ That's a good point. We can talk about that next time though. ▶ I'm afraid that we're going to run out of time if we don't move on. We only have [a few minutes left].
g Telling someone you can't hear them*	▶ I'm sorry. I didn't hear you. ▶ Can you say that a little louder, please? ▶ Sorry! What did you say?
h Telling someone they speak too fast*	▶ I'm sorry. Can you say that a little slower? ▶ Can you please slow down? ▶ Sorry. I didn't catch what you said.

*You can also use clarification strategies to make sure you understood someone who is quiet or talks too quickly.

Discussion strategies

2 Clarifying

Sometimes it is hard for you to understand what someone is saying or for others to understand you. Clarifying is a natural part of discussions. Even native speakers use these strategies because not everyone understands everything all the time!

Clarification strategies	Sample phrases	Examples
a Clarifying (when you didn't understand someone else)	Sorry, but I don't understand. I'm not sure what you mean by that. I didn't follow what you said. I'm not sure what you're getting at.	
b Restating (when someone doesn't understand you)	In other words . . .	**A:** We need to read and correctly interpret body language to understand someone fully. **B:** I'm not sure what you mean by that. **A:** In other words, we need to become more aware of the different messages that body language communicates.
	By that, I mean . . .	**A:** Good persuaders use pathos. **B:** I'm not sure what you mean by pathos. **A:** By that, I mean using emotions. Good persuaders appeal to their audience's emotional state.
c Checking (when you want to make sure someone understands you)	Just checking—do you know what I mean? Is that clear? Does anyone have any questions? Does that make sense?	
d Paraphrasing (what the speaker says)	Are you saying that . . .	**A:** A quick decision is not always a bad decision. **B:** Are you saying that it depends on what type of decision it is more than how long it takes us to make the decision?
	Do you mean that . . .	**A:** I think we should follow the seven steps in the decision-making process. **B:** Do you mean that following the seven steps will lead to better results?
e Paraphrasing (what someone else says)	Jing said that . . .	Jing said that when we're connected and engaged, we're more likely to have fun and restore our energy levels.
	What . . . means is . . .	What Alberto means is that switching our attention between two things can lead to neither of them being done well.

Discussion strategies

3 Getting involved

It can be challenging to participate in discussions. Sometimes you have to involve yourself without being asked, keep your turn (if others try to interrupt you), interrupt (when others are talking), and get your turn back (after being interrupted).

Participation strategies	Sample phrases	Examples
a Getting involved	▶ Can I ask a question? ▶ I have something I'd like to contribute. ▶ I can offer some input on this topic.	
b Keeping your turn	▶ Excuse me, but I'd just like to finish this one idea. ▶ Sorry, but could you give me one more second to finish? ▶ It won't take me long to finish this thought.	
c Interrupting	Excuse me . . . Sorry to interrupt . . . Can I add to . . .	▶ Excuse me, but I'd like to add another idea. ▶ Sorry to interrupt, but I have a question. ▶ Can I add to what you just said?
d Getting your turn back	As I was saying . . . Going back to what I was saying before . . . In any case . . .	▶ As I was saying, multi-tasking is not necessarily a good thing to do. ▶ Going back to what I was saying before, choose tasks that don't distract from each other. ▶ In any case, people need to know how much attention each task needs.
e Commenting (on what someone has said)	That's a good point . . . I see what you mean . . . I'm sorry, but I disagree.	▶ That's a good point, Julia. ▶ I see what you mean, Eric. ▶ I'm sorry, but I disagree.
f Adding (to what someone has said)	I agree with you . . . and also . . . Another thing to consider is . . . I have something to add to that . . .	▶ I agree with you about elevator pitches needing to be persuasive, Carlos. And also, I think we need to remember to keep them to 30 seconds. ▶ Yes, and another thing to consider is how to approach potential employers. ▶ What Carlos said is true, and I have something to add to that.

Discussion strategies

4 Organizing

Lastly, organization techniques can help communication and make discussion easier to follow.

Organization technique	Sample words and phrases	Examples
a Chronological	First . . . second . . . third . . . Next . . . then . . . later	First, let's talk about how you can differentiate yourself from others. Second, we'll discuss how to list your main strengths and key skills. Third, we'll add these ideas to your profile. Next, we'll talk about dress codes in the workplace. Then, we'll talk about work hours. Later, we'll discuss company culture.
b Cause and effect	If . . ., then . . . When . . ., then . . .	If you read a company's website, then you're able to find out a lot about the company's culture. When you read about a company on its website, then you are able to better prepare for an interview.
c Categorical	There are five strategies . . . The main things . . .	There are five strategies for meeting deadlines. The main thing to do is to set deadline reminders.
d Problem and solution	The main problem is . . . One big issue is . . . The best solution is . . . We could . . .	The main problem is that we aren't managing our time well. One big issue is we don't allow for delays when we set deadlines. The best solution is to allow for delays when we set deadlines. We could brainstorm ideas and then discuss which one is best.
e Adding an idea	On top of that . . . In the same way . . .	There are personal benefits to having deadlines. On top of that, there are many professional benefits to having deadlines. Pitches are used in sales and advertising to refer to a short speech that tries to persuade someone to buy something. In the same way, an elevator pitch is a short speech that tries to persuade someone to hire you.
f Contrast	Although . . . However . . .	Although verbal communication is very important, nonverbal communication is equally powerful. People sometimes cross their arms during a conversation. However, this often gives the impression that someone is not interested in, or open to, what the other people are saying.

VOCABULARY PRACTICE

Vocabulary practice 1

Exercise (A)

Complete the puzzle.

Across

2 having or showing true feelings that are expressed in an honest way
4 to not have the same traits or characteristics
7 not certain or having doubts
10 favored
11 to state or show very strongly that you have particular rights or powers

Down

1 to believe that someone's behavior, words, or an event have a particular meaning
3 the action or process of conveying something
5 giving attention and effort to a specific task or goal
6 the lines of hair that grow over your eyes
8 a serious facial expression that usually shows anger, displeasure, or concentration
9 to discover or notice the presence of something that is hidden or hard to see, hear, taste, smell

Exercise (B)

Use the correct words from the puzzle to complete the dialogue.

Look. Diane's talking to the new HR director. She doesn't seem very happy.

Why do you say that?

Look at her 1 __________. She always raises them when she disapproves of something.

I don't 2 __________ it that way. She could just be surprised.

But her forehead is wrinkled, too.

Maybe she's just 3 __________ on their conversation. See, she's smiling now.

I can 4 __________ a fake smile when I see one—and that is one.

Now, she's tapping her fingers. What does that mean?

She's either nervous or 5 __________ of herself.

Well, the meaning of gestures may 6 __________ from person to person.

Vocabulary practice 2

Exercise (A)

Complete the puzzle. What is the vertical word?

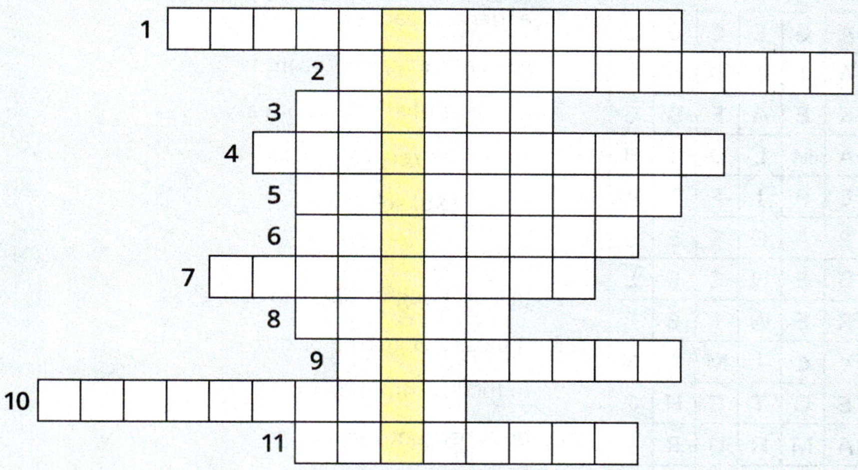

1 one who makes money by starting their own business
2 a quality of warmth that makes you feel welcome and comfortable
3 to cause someone to do something
4 to describe a person that you can depend on
5 to understand others' feelings
6 possible to believe
7 unwilling, unenthusiastic
8 to try to persuade somebody to buy something
9 pleasant and easy to get along with
10 convincing
11 a short account of a humorous incident

Exercise (B)

Use the correct words from the puzzle to complete the recommendation letter below.

<u>Recommendation for Tom Johnson</u>

To whom it may concern,

Tom has been my personal assistant for the last six years. He has been in charge of handling confidential records, and I can honestly say that he is one of the most [1] ____________ employees I have ever worked with. He's also extremely [2] ____________ and a very popular team member. Colleagues and clients often comment on his [3] ____________. He is able to [4] ____________ with people and understand how they feel. Tom always comes up with great ideas and he is very [5] ____________ when communicating those ideas to others, and usually gets people to support him. Tom would definitely be an asset to any [6] ____________ employer.

Sincerely,
Melanie Rodriguez
Manager

Vocabulary practice 3

Exercise A

Read the clues and find the words.

W	P	B	H	R	S	A	B	O	T	A	G	E	C	O	Z
P	R	O	C	R	A	S	T	I	N	A	T	I	O	N	E
C	K	Q	H	A	G	E	P	M	E	K	E	A	F	D	C
A	U	P	A	Y	O	F	F	O	D	A	M	L	D	U	H
R	N	E	W	P	L	A	M	K	I	E	P	I	F	R	A
J	H	S	D	O	Y	N	E	T	L	P	A	G	S	S	L
B	S	E	L	F	C	O	N	F	I	D	E	N	C	E	L
O	E	L	N	P	R	E	S	S	U	R	E	W	I	E	E
A	L	F	Y	R	E	B	U	D	D	Y	C	I	M	T	N
C	F	T	H	A	S	S	E	C	X	E	O	T	G	H	G
T	T	A	S	T	I	C	K	T	O	A	M	H	U	R	I
I	O	L	S	E	L	O	H	R	E	P	M	A	D	O	N
O	W	K	A	M	I	A	P	I	R	E	I	S	V	U	G
N	K	D	R	I	E	M	E	S	D	S	T	I	C	G	O
S	A	B	O	T	N	L	W	U	N	X	O	T	I	H	A
S	F	I	R	S	T	O	H	G	U	I	D	E	F	N	L

1 a friend, a partner
2 gain, advantage, or profit
3 opposite of effortless or easy
4 be able to recover quickly
5 opposite of self-doubt
6 force
7 talk or thoughts directed at oneself
8 opposite of give up or quit
9 to fulfill a commitment
10 be consistent with
11 to disrupt, to hinder

Exercise B

Use the correct words from the puzzle to complete Sarah's diary.

Monday
I planned out my whole week. I have to [1] ______________ my schedule to finish my design on time!

Tuesday
I got distracted and already managed to [2] ______________ my plan to finish the second draft by today. Now I have to stop all the negative [3] ______________ in my head!

Wednesday
Gina is putting a lot of [4] ______________ on me. She's constantly asking if I have finished!

Thursday
I finally completed the design— and the team loved it, including Gina! Her comments really boosted my [5] ______________!

Friday
At dinner tonight, I told Peter I want to take a dance class, and he offered to be my dance [6] ______________. We're starting lessons next week!

Saturday
It was such a [7] ______________ week, but I got through it— and the [8] ______________ was worth it. So proud of myself!

Vocabulary practice 4

Exercise (A)

Complete the puzzle.

Across

3 We're working on a campaign to raise ___________ about the seriousness of the issue.

4 After all our hard work, it was very ___________ when the project was a success.

6 There is a clear ___________ between the departments; they need to work together to succeed.

8 We need to listen to and clarify the needs of the team to ___________ the current conflict.

10 If you improve your observation skills, you'll be able to better ___________ the feelings of people around you.

Down

1 As it was her first day in the office, Tracy was ___________ to join her colleagues for lunch.

2 Team members who ___________ aggressive and defensive behavior are less successful than the rest of the group.

5 ___________ motivation is the act of doing something for your own satisfaction rather than for external rewards.

7 Giving ___________ boosts motivation and reinforces positive behavior.

9 Try to find a job that will ___________ you to get up in the morning with enthusiasm.

Exercise (B)

Use the correct words from the puzzle to complete the notes taken during a talk on emotional intelligence.

EMOTIONAL INTELLIGENCE (EQ)

- Ability to:
  - understand + manage own emotions
  - try to [1] ___________ the emotions of others + empathize (How? Develop emotional [2] ___________)
- Why important for teams?
  - helps members understand the [3] ___________ they have with each other
  - helps to [4] ___________ conflicts
  - fuels team members' [5] ___________ motivation
  - results in a more [6] ___________ experience

Vocabulary practice 5

Exercise A

Complete the puzzle. What is the vertical word?

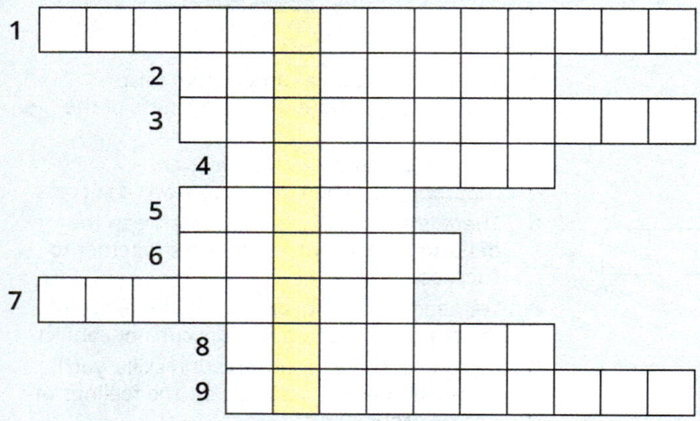

1 If you want others to hear your ideas, you need to be part of the ______________.

2 When you ______________ a job offer, it's important to think about more than just the amount of money you'll make.

3 This suggestion won't work. Can you propose a(n) ______________?

4 The ______________ will depend on a number of factors, so it's not easy to predict it.

5 They need to ______________ the advantages and disadvantages of each option before making a choice.

6 After they ______________ the survey responses, they'll analyze them and present the results.

7 Even though it can be frightening, we all sometimes need to make ______________ decisions.

8 Decisions that have an insignificant impact are ______________.

9 The fact that Peter was ______________ about which supplier to use significantly slowed the process down.

Exercise B

Use the correct words from the puzzle to complete the questions. Then take the quiz.

Are you a good decision maker? Take the quiz!

How often do you . . .	Always (2 points)	Sometimes (1 point)	Never (0 points)
• first determine whether it is a low-risk or [1] ______________ decision?	☐	☐	☐
• [2] ______________ data and research related to a project?	☐	☐	☐
• [3] ______________ the pros and cons of each option?	☐	☐	☐
• evaluate more than one [4] ______________ of each option before making a choice?	☐	☐	☐
• look for a(n) [5] ______________ if you don't like the current options?	☐	☐	☐
• avoid being [6] ______________ and act on the decision?	☐	☐	☐

Add up your points:

10–12: You're good at making decisions!

5–9: You're not bad at making decisions.

0–4: You can improve your decision making.

Vocabulary practice 6

Exercise (A)

Read the clues and find the words.

M	A	S	A	L	I	T	U	R	N	O	V	E	R	C	B
I	Z	A	U	Q	S	E	U	J	A	T	L	S	M	Z	E
N	C	K	T	C	H	A	R	I	S	M	A	T	I	C	B
F	O	I	O	A	O	G	Z	W	I	U	A	E	H	O	L
R	M	E	N	T	O	R	I	N	G	E	D	I	Y	N	M
A	M	Z	O	R	K	L	N	O	U	R	E	H	A	S	U
N	I	B	M	A	M	A	N	I	P	U	L	A	T	E	Z
J	T	O	Y	B	U	R	N	O	U	T	E	N	F	N	B
O	M	M	I	H	D	P	B	T	H	U	G	D	L	S	O
N	E	G	L	E	C	T	E	D	A	N	A	S	E	U	O
B	N	A	R	D	O	M	I	N	A	N	T	O	X	S	S
R	T	L	I	S	L	A	P	A	T	E	E	F	E	H	T
U	P	L	E	A	D	E	R	Y	I	B	W	F	D	N	U
T	U	S	A	Y	K	E	X	J	B	U	O	G	Q	O	R
A	A	U	T	H	O	R	I	T	A	R	I	A	N	A	P
F	I	R	S	G	H	U	N	V	K	O	B	T	S	C	O

1 She was a very ____________ CEO who always controlled the conversation at meetings.

2 Giving positive feedback is a great way to ____________ employee morale.

3 They accused him of trying to ____________ people and of misusing his power.

4 Jessie had been working alone for almost ten years, so she found it hard to ____________ her duties to her new assistant.

5 Companies seek employees who show ____________ and dedication to the company's success.

6 ____________ leadership involves taking absolute control over a task or group.

7 During ____________ sessions, experienced employees help new staff members by giving them advice and sharing knowledge.

8 We have a ____________ manager; he empowers us to take initiative instead of telling us what to do all the time.

9 It took several hours for the project team to reach a ____________ about how to proceed with the prototype.

10 Increased ____________ at work is known to increase employees' motivation, creativity, and happiness.

11 All the team members are fond of his magnetic personality and charm; he is the most ____________ team leader we've ever had.

12 The team felt ____________ when they found out that their manager had not included them in the decision making.

Exercise (B)

Use the correct words from the puzzle to complete the comments of employees on a blog post.

Danielle: Although [1]____________ managers can be bossy, I like being told what to do. It makes my life easier.

Anders: I work best with managers who have a(n) [2]____________ approach, so I can be more creative. I don't like managers who constantly look over my shoulder.

Martina: I agree with you, Anders! Having [3]____________ at work is a big priority for me. When I'm given freedom at work, I'm more productive.

Akhil: I appreciate managers who work hard toward getting general [4]____________ on the team so that everyone is in agreement.

Jada: I know what you mean, Akhil. I honestly feel ignored or [5]____________ when I'm not asked for my opinion at work.

Kazue: For me, the best manager is the one who prioritizes my growth and acknowledges my successes. It really helps to affirm my [6]____________ to my job and my company.

Vocabulary practice 7

Exercise A

Complete the puzzle. What is the vertical word?

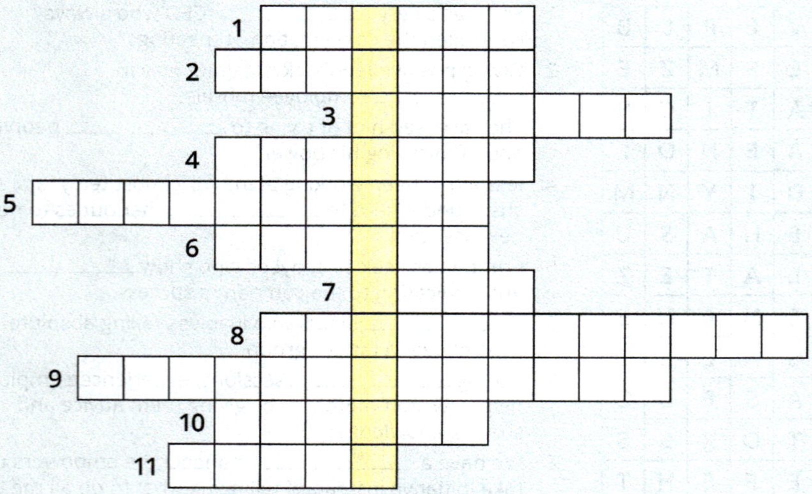

1 to develop the ability to do something well
2 temporary
3 threatening to happen soon
4 a problem or difficulty
5 to classify, group
6 to put forward for approval or consideration
7 speed
8 the quality or state of being able to generate or create
9 to think something has less value than it actually does
10 to make it last longer than before or end at a later date
11 to fear

Exercise B

Use the correct words from the puzzle to complete the dialogue between two colleagues.

Hi, Josh. You look worried. Is everything OK?

I have to 1 __________ my report by tomorrow morning, and I don't know how I'm going to get it done.

Why did you leave it to the last minute?

Well, I always manage to 2 __________ how long it will take and then run out of time. Now the deadline is 3 __________ over me. I tried to 4 __________ the data into sections to make it clearer, but now it looks more complicated.

How about asking them to 5 __________ the deadline?

Unfortunately, I can't. My manager needs it for a meeting with a client first thing tomorrow.

Well then, maybe I can help but, in future, you'll need to think about your time management to improve your 6 __________.

Wow, Wendy, thanks so much. You're the best! I owe you one.

Vocabulary practice 8

Exercise (A)

Read the clues and find the words.

S	D	E	T	R	I	X	O	M	E	N	P	S	C	L	O
H	B	L	U	R	A	S	J	Q	B	U	R	D	D	O	B
I	Y	B	E	Z	O	N	E	U	U	D	O	Q	E	S	L
Z	B	U	R	D	E	N	M	V	R	I	S	B	S	A	U
T	U	D	E	T	R	I	M	E	N	T	A	L	I	K	P
A	R	I	T	B	A	M	E	T	O	X	G	J	G	M	K
W	D	L	Z	O	Y	B	Z	R	U	O	R	A	N	E	R
D	S	U	M	U	T	A	J	A	T	A	P	T	A	N	E
E	N	E	R	Q	U	L	A	P	T	C	W	I	T	M	W
M	S	A	E	N	S	A	L	E	I	S	U	R	E	D	A
A	O	N	W	O	K	N	L	D	A	T	S	S	U	L	R
N	Y	E	A	L	N	C	E	O	D	R	A	I	N	E	D
D	R	E	C	O	R	E	T	C	O	P	K	M	E	Z	E
S	H	I	F	T	O	S	P	E	C	I	A	L	I	S	T
L	Z	U	T	S	L	E	E	P	L	E	S	S	A	U	G
U	P	Y	A	M	E	N	E	R	G	I	Z	E	C	O	N

1 Too much stress is ______________ to your health.

2 We prioritize the clients' ______________ in order to meet their expectations.

3 When I'm stressed, my manager always says things to ______________ me and make me enjoy my work again.

4 Veronica felt so ______________ that as soon as she got home, she went straight to bed.

5 It is motivating for employees when you ______________ them for the extra hours they work.

6 Managing a big team can be very stressful, and many team leaders eventually suffer ______________.

7 Because of a(n) ______________ of power, she wasn't able to make as many decisions as her co-director.

8 To build his confidence, Frank has to learn to ______________ his focus away from the negative thoughts he has about himself.

9 She tends to ______________ the distinction between her private and professional life and often says the wrong things in meetings.

Exercise (B)

Use the correct words from the puzzle to complete Nancy's email to her mentor.

Email

Nancy Johnson
To: Bill Davis
Subject: Thank you

Dear Bill,

After we spoke, I decided to take your advice and found a new job in an effort to improve my physical and mental health. I started working at a new company a few weeks ago. Now I can see clearly that it was the 1 ______________ between my work and home life which made me feel 2 ______________ all the time. How exhausting! I'll never 3 ______________ my private and professional life again. Now, when I get home after work, I 4 ______________ my attention away from work and toward my personal well-being. I 5 ______________ myself by socializing with family and friends, and I never forget to 6 ______________ myself whenever I achieve one of my goals. You've had such a profound influence on my career and my private life.

Thank you very much.

Nancy Johnson

Vocabulary practice 9

Exercise A

Complete the puzzle.

Across

6 They will be subject to a new ______________ of conduct and will be monitored by authorities more frequently.

7 I admire my coach for his ______________, so I always try to uphold his moral values for our team.

8 Everyone in the office counts on the ______________ of our manager. He always treats people equally.

9 He used another writer's words and ideas in his essay without giving him any credit, and the professor said that it wasn't a(n) ______________ to do.

11 All workers must be treated with ______________ and respect.

Down

1 They are expected to be ______________ about the process and will share how they reached their decision.

2 The ______________ was resolved thanks to the team manager's suggestion.

3 The proposal wasn't ______________. It would have reduced our profit margin significantly, so we rejected it.

4 You shouldn't make a(n) ______________ until you get all the information. You don't want to make the wrong decision.

5 They were offered a(n) ______________ to keep quiet about what they had witnessed.

10 You know what they say: "______________ is the best policy." If I were you, I'd tell the truth.

Exercise B

Use the correct words from the puzzle to complete the text.

1

They tried to offer me a(n) 1 ______________ to give their company the contract.

That's not very 2 ______________. You don't want to do business with people like that!

2

Senior management is not at all 3 ______________. We have no idea what they plan to do next.

That's not great. I believe all companies should have a(n) 4 ______________ regarding how decisions are made.

3

I have a(n) 5 ______________ regarding which product to launch the company with. I just can't decide.

Well, you need to start making as much profit as possible at the beginning, so choose the most 6 ______________ one.

4

Apparently, he's not known for his 7 ______________ in doing business. He says whatever he needs to in order to close the deal.

Don't listen to others. Speak to him yourself and make your own 8 ______________.

Vocabulary practice 10

Exercise (A)

Read the clues and find the words.

R	E	C	R	U	I	T	M	E	N	T	F	A	I	R
T	P	O	T	E	N	T	I	A	L	I	N	U	T	E
E	X	M	H	E	L	P	I	N	R	P	I	T	C	H
R	P	E	A	C	O	R	A	T	A	R	G	H	T	E
C	K	A	V	Q	U	I	Y	A	R	T	I	E	O	A
V	I	C	R	A	F	T	I	R	E	A	L	N	P	R
B	N	R	O	A	R	I	M	G	A	P	E	T	E	S
N	J	O	B	S	E	E	K	E	R	O	K	I	N	E
O	G	S	W	I	N	T	E	T	O	W	E	C	I	P
P	O	S	T	H	E	N	T	I	C	I	R	E	N	I
Q	V	R	E	H	J	A	C	R	O	N	L	H	G	T
A	N	E	T	W	O	R	K	S	S	N	I	E	N	C
F	O	F	F	E	B	F	A	I	R	I	K	A	O	K
D	R	S	E	E	K	E	R	J	O	N	E	O	F	F
E	L	E	V	A	T	O	R	N	T	G	R	R	W	H

1 an event where people search for a job
2 to practice before the main event
3 how you seem to someone else
4 to shape with skill
5 a person looking for work
6 the things one says to convince others to buy or invest in something
7 to aim something at a specific group of people
8 limited to a single time
9 genuine, real
10 leading to success

Exercise (B)

Use the correct words from the puzzle to complete the event flyer.

Are you a [1] ______________ struggling to find work?

Have you ever thought of attending a [2] ______________?

Why not come along to the

Career Fair Prep Night!

Tired of the same old cliché career advice from non-experts?

Come and get [3] ______________ tips that will help you succeed from [4] ______________ employment recruiters and professional career advisors.

Don't want to miss another opportunity?

Learn how to polish and [5] ______________ your elevator [6] ______________.

Want to gain confidence?

[7] ______________ in role plays until you're perfect at the next interview you attend!

Don't miss this [8] ______________ opportunity!

Friday, September 6th, 6–8 p.m., Main Building

Vocabulary practice 11

Exercise A

Complete the puzzle.

Across

3 It's difficult to ________ between the original brand and its imitators.

7 A ________ program was created based on the requirements of the client.

10 Why don't you ask people in your network to ________ you for the skills you have?

11 You need to ________ your résumé to match the job description.

12 If you're looking for a job, it's wise to check the ________ websites for recruiters.

Down

1 You need to be more ________ when there's a problem so that it doesn't get worse.

2 They decided to ________ extra part-time staff to assist customers during the holiday rush.

4 People ________ much of their knowledge through their experiences and failures.

5 The main aim of the exhibition is to ________ the work of local artists.

6 Derek visits the branch offices ________ to ensure that everything is on track.

8 You need to keep your résumé ________ by adding your latest work experiences.

9 You can call me ________ at this number; it's for my personal cell phone.

Exercise B

Use the correct words from the puzzle to complete the tips.

Today's Top Tips for Jobseekers!

Check the [1] ________ sites for your area of work.

- ☐ Do research on the company that is looking to [2] ________ you.
- ☐ Have references that [3] ________ your achievements.
- ☐ Make sure your résumé is [4] ________ with your latest achievements.
- ☐ Prepare [5] ________ cover letters and [6] ________ your résumé for each position.
- ☐ Think about what will [7] ________ you from the other candidates.
- ☐ Attend education or training programs to [8] ________ new skills.

Vocabulary practice 12

Exercise A

Read the clues and find the words or phrases.

Across

1 The company is not a(n) __________ one, but I have no doubt that they will be successful.

5 Although Will earns very little, he manages to __________ by splitting rent with a roommate.

7 The aim of this course is to __________ people with the skills necessary for a job.

9 The cost of __________ at the university has increased significantly in the last few years.

10 After evaluating the __________, we decided to accept the offer.

Down

2 __________ health insurance was one of the most appealing aspects of the company's offer.

3 After almost a year of __________, the company had hired a dream team of scientists.

4 Janet accepted the job because she believes she can contribute __________ to the company's mission of feeding the hungry.

6 The idea of working as a teacher and having the summers off is very __________ to me.

8 Our consultant is a woman with considerable __________ into local politics.

Exercise B

Use the correct words from the puzzle to complete the dialog.

Tracy: So, have you made up your mind about your career plan?

Mandy: Well, I [1]__________ thought about all the risks, and I've decided to quit my job.

Tracy: Wow! Are you sure? The company you work for is a very [2]__________ one, and you have a lot of great [3]__________ there, like sick pay and annual leave.

Mandy: I know, but being a musician is very [4]__________ to me. It's what I've always wanted to do. I want to [5]__________ myself with the necessary skills to pursue a career in music.

Tracy: I see. But without pay, how will you [6]__________?

Mandy: I've saved enough to get by, and I'll find a part-time job which won't take so much time away from my music.

Tracy: Well, it sounds like you've got a plan. Good luck.

Glossary

Module 1: Communication 1

disrespect (n) lack of respect for someone or something
index finger (n) the finger next to your thumb
summon (v) to order someone to come to a place

Module 2: Communication 2

dilute (v) to make a quality, belief etc. weaker or less effective
roam (v) to walk or travel, usually for a long time, with no clear purpose or direction
unappetizing (adj) food that has an unattractive appearance and that makes you think it will not taste good

Module 3: Goal Setting

3D (adj) a 3D film or picture is made so that it appears to have length, width, and depth, and therefore the people and things in it look much more real. 3D is short for "three dimensional"
advancement (n) progress or development in your job, level of knowledge, etc.
keep up with (phr v) to write to, telephone, or meet a friend regularly, so that you do not forget each other

Module 4: Teamwork

accounting (n) the work of keeping a company's financial records, recording its income and expenses, and its business deals
anonymously (adv) doing something without being known

Module 5: Critical Thinking

overthink (v) to think about something too much, which is not useful
stuck (adj) impossible or unable to move from a certain position

Module 6: Leadership

aggressively (adv) in a determined way
downsize (v) if a company or organization downsizes, it reduces the number of people it employs in order to reduce costs
guru (n) 1. someone who knows a lot about a particular subject, and gives advice to other people 2. a Hindu religious teacher or leader

Module 7: Self-Management

back out (phr v) to decide not to do something that you had promised to do
brush up (phr v) to practice and improve your skills or your knowledge of something that you learned in the past
pop up (phr v) to appear, sometimes unexpectedly

Module 8: Wellness

allocate (v) to use something for a particular purpose, give something to a particular person etc., especially after an official decision has been made
confidentially (adv) a way of speaking or behaving that shows you do not want other people to know what you are saying
prioritize (v) to put several things, problems, etc. in order of importance, so that you deal with the most important ones first

Module 9: Social Responsibility

compliance program (n) a set of internal policies and procedures within a company to comply with laws, rules, and regulations
mark up (phr v) to increase the price of something, so that you sell it for more than you paid for it
merger (n) the joining together of two or more companies or organizations to form one larger one

Module 10: Branding

automated (adj) using computers and machines to do a job, rather than people
culinary (adj) relating to cooking
funnel (n) a channel which allows sending money, information etc. from various places to someone
impeccable (adj) without any faults and impossible to criticize
notion (n) an idea, belief, or opinion

Module 11: Job Search

blend (n) a mixture of different things that combine together well
go beyond (phr v) to be much better, worse, more serious etc. than something else

Module 12: Interviewing

associate (n) someone who you work with or do business with
in-house (adj) working within a company or organization
quarterly (adj) produced or happening four times a year

Notes